GLOBALIZATION
AND TERRORISM

GLOBALIZATION

Series Editors
Manfred B. Steger
*Royal Melbourne Institute of Technology and
University of Hawai'i–Mānoa*
and
Terrell Carver
University of Bristol

"Globalization" has become *the* buzzword of our time. But what does it mean? Rather than forcing a complicated social phenomenon into a single analytical framework, this series seeks to present globalization as a multidimensional process constituted by complex, often contradictory interactions of global, regional, and local aspects of social life. Since conventional disciplinary borders and lines of demarcation are losing their old rationales in a globalizing world, authors in this series apply an interdisciplinary framework to the study of globalization. In short, the main purpose and objective of this series is to support subject-specific inquiries into the dynamics and effects of contemporary globalization and its varying impacts across, between, and within societies.

 Supported by the Globalization Research Center at the University of Hawai'i, Mānoa

GLOBALIZATION AND TERRORISM

THE MIGRATION OF DREAMS AND NIGHTMARES

SECOND EDITION

JAMAL R. NASSAR

ROWMAN & LITTLEFIELD PUBLISHERS, INC.
Lanham • Boulder • New York • Toronto • Plymouth, UK

ROWMAN & LITTLEFIELD PUBLISHERS, INC.

Published in the United States of America
by Rowman & Littlefield Publishers, Inc.
A wholly owned subsidiary of The Rowman & Littlefield Publishing Group, Inc.
4501 Forbes Boulevard, Suite 200, Lanham, Maryland 20706
www.rowmanlittlefield.com

Estover Road, Plymouth PL6 7PY, United Kingdom

British Library Cataloguing in Publication Information Available

Library of Congress Cataloging-in-Publication Data

Nassar, Jamal R. (Jamal Raji)
  Globalization and terrorism : the migration of dreams and nightmares / Jamal R.
Nassar. — 2nd ed.
     p. cm. — (Globalization)
  Includes bibliographical references and index.
  ISBN 978-0-7425-5787-1 (cloth : alk. paper) — ISBN 978-0-7425-5788-8 (pbk. :
alk. paper) — ISBN 978-0-7425-5789-5 (electronic)
  1. Terrorism and globalization. I. Title.
  HV6431.N38 2010
  363.325—dc22   2009010510

Printed in the United States of America

⊚™The paper used in this publication meets the minimum requirements of
American National Standard for Information Sciences—Permanence of Paper
for Printed Library Materials, ANSI/NISO Z39.48-1992.

CONTENTS

PREFACE

Since the publication of the first edition of this book, globalization and terrorism have both taken a leap forward. Globalization has continued at a fast pace. Any individual who purchased fuel in the summer of 2008 has noticed the impact of globalization at the pump. Equally true has been the growth and fear of terrorism. The December 2008 attacks on several sites in Mumbai, India, as well as the increased piracy near the Somali coast, are clear indications that terror has become a regular fact of life. Terror and globalization are old but the speed of their growth and development is new. The fall 2008 financial crises have highlighted the globalization of economies everywhere. The bank failures and falling stock values have terrorized many people around the globe. Eventually, the poor will pay the price as economic woes of the rich will migrate to the wretched of the earth. They, in turn, will respond not only with despair but perhaps with a new wave of violence that will migrate to the rich. Globalization and terrorism are, in essence, intertwined.

A former student of mine wrote me one of those rare but special notes that teachers occasionally receive. Lynn Weddle of the class of 1985 wrote, "I often am reminded of the many things I learned while in your class and how some of the things you mentioned became truly prophetic." My former student went on to remind me of a statement I had made in class arguing that the Soviet Union was not the enemy we needed to fear but rather "a Third World country that we would never expect to wreak havoc on the U.S." The events of September 11, 2001, reminded her of that statement. While the terror of that dreadful day was a wake-up call to most Americans, it has been a normal way of life for a long time to many people around the world. It certainly has been a part of my life since birth.

When I was born in Jerusalem in 1946, the city was in the midst of a terror campaign. My pregnant mother had to walk a few blocks in the midst of curfew to reach the hospital. On the way, British soldiers stopped her and frisked her to make sure that she was pregnant with me rather than hiding a bomb. The terror groups of those days had such names as Irgun and Stern rather than al Qaeda or Hamas. Their leaders were such individuals as Menachem Begin, Yitzhak Shamir, and Erik Sharon. Since my birth, the terror there has never stopped. The Palestinians became dispossessed, and the Israelis became independent and strong. Whenever in despair, the Palestinians themselves came to wage new waves of terror.

Just like terror, globalization has been a part of my life all along. I was born in Palestine as a British subject. I grew up on the West Bank as a Jordanian one. My family continues to live there as Israeli ones. I am a citizen of the United States. My brother and his family are Swedish. I had a sister who was Lebanese and a niece who is French. A nephew of mine is Venezuelan. I have cousins who live the world over. When the World Trade Center was attacked, a distant cousin perished in the ashes of that dreadful day. Borders have come to mean unpleasant barriers rather than permanent fixtures.

Given my background, when the series editors, Professors Manfred Steger and Terrell Carver, asked me to author a book on globalization and terrorism, I did not hesitate to accept. I felt that I had something to say. Little did I know what I had gotten myself into. Both globalization and terrorism are complex and difficult subjects. Neither has a simple definition or an agreed-on trend. After all, globalization is both a blessing and a curse. Terrorism, likewise, is in the eye of the beholder. A terrorist is such to her enemies and a freedom fighter to her friends. To some, the terrorist may be the corporate chief executive officer or a president of a country. To most in the United States, the image of the terrorist is that of some wild-eyed Muslim dedicated to some apocalyptic vision of a clash between the "civilized world" and Islam. In this book, I present globalization and terrorism for what they are, not what some may wish them to be.

ACKNOWLEDGMENTS

This work could not have been done without the guidance, assistance, and encouragement of many individuals. First and foremost, I want to thank Professor Manfred Steger for his continuous support of the project. Professor Steger read many drafts and made numerous suggestions. He was always there to help with an idea or to just listen to my frustrations. Professor Steger is a true friend and a giant scholar. His series coeditor, Professor Terrell Carver, was also patient and understanding. I could not have dreamt of better series editors to work with. Susan McEachern, Editorial Director at Rowman & Littlefield, was very helpful in the process of producing the second edition of the book. Robin Bewley did a wonderful job helping me put together this edition. For the original edition, Jennifer Knerr of Rowman & Littlefield believed in me when I had doubts myself. Her suggestions and her persistence made this work presentable. For that edition, my graduate assistants, Suzanne Daddy and Anthony DiMaggio, did a superb job in helping me. Anthony was a dedicated assistant whose persistence contributed to making this work better. His hard work and dedication leave me indebted to him forever. Finally, a word of thanks must be added to my wife, Hanan, and my children, Sami and Gina, for putting up with me when I was under the pressure to complete and revise the manuscript.

INTRODUCTION

A basic theme that runs through this book is the notion of *migration of dreams*. As some people advance, leaving others behind, they export dreams to them. The dreams of the underdog occasionally transform themselves into nightmares for those who are perceived to be an obstacle to the fulfillment of dreams. This cycle of dreams and nightmares is enhanced by globalization and effected by terrorism. Some concrete cases are presented in the book to show how dreams and nightmares interact in this globalized and terrorized world of ours.

Chapter 1 attempts to set the stage for the book. It presents globalization as a concept and in practice. Terrorism is also introduced as an inaccurate concept that lacks an acceptable definition. The link between globalization and terrorism is discussed, and the concepts of migration of dreams and *migration of nightmares* are presented as the merging points of both globalization and terrorism. Globalization contributes to dreams among those who are poor or oppressed. Dreams enlarge the gap between expectations and achievements. This gap contributes to violence that often migrates to the lands of the rich and powerful. It is this cycle of dreams and nightmares that characterizes our globalized world today.

Chapter 2 takes a hard look at the root causes of terrorism. It argues that the major motivation for terrorist violence is the struggle for power and justice. The desperate and oppressed want justice. The rich and powerful want more wealth and power. The clash between them brings nightmares of violence and terror to both.

Chapter 3 investigates Palestinian terrorism by looking at its root causes. It sets the historical background of the conflict between Israelis and Palestinians and explains the violence of both. Palestinian dispossession and Israeli thirst for power have created a violent atmosphere where the dreams of one become the nightmares of the other. Thus, dreams and nightmares begin to migrate between both societies. That cycle continues without an end in sight.

Chapter 4 reviews globalization and terrorism in other regional conflicts. The conflict in Northern Ireland is assessed as another case of the imperial drive for power leading to dispossession and violence. Similar conflicts in Colombia, Chechnya, Iraq, Afghanistan, and Congo are assessed with similar conclusions. The drive of the powerful for more wealth and power brings violence to the weak. The weak, in turn, carry out violent terror against their perceived oppressors.

Chapter 5 explains Islamist terrorism in the context of its origins in the struggle against colonialism. Egyptian and Saudi Islamists merged in the Afghani struggle against Soviet domination there. With the help of the United States, they eventually succeeded. The struggle to defeat imperial designs against Muslims did not end with the end of Soviet occupation of Afghanistan. Soon after, the struggle for power moved to Iraq; it also continued in Chechnya, Bosnia, Serbia, Palestine, Saudi Arabia, and a host of other places where Islamist leaders perceived an injustice against Muslims to exist. Consequently, a clash between the United States and Islamists produced more violence and terror. That cycle continues until this day.

The final chapter attempts to pull these threads together. It also tries to look into the future with an eye for possibilities. Globalization and terrorism are discussed as interlinked developments. The nightmare of terrorism is discussed as a product of the globalized dreams for a more equitable world. The clash between the two should be turned into a dialogue among the powerful and the weak. Without hope for those weak and oppressed, violence is likely to continue.

CHAPTER 1

GLOBALIZATION AND TERRORISM

The terrorist attacks of September 11, 2001, and the subsequent wars in Afghanistan and Iraq crystallized the need for thorough, high quality, and innovative research and analysis of the issues of globalization and terrorism. The world today is very different from the world our grandparents lived in. It is much more connected and, perhaps, much more dangerous. It is, however, still essentially the same world with similar forces of dominance and challenge. Those who are dominated challenge those who dominate. Naturally, when "Rome" is attacked, it responds with deadly force. This book will not discuss globalization and terrorism from the perspective of the dominant powers only but will also introduce the views of those who are dominated by them. History, after all, is full of examples where victims learned the discourse of oppression from those who oppressed them. History has many examples of victims who are portrayed as aggressors and aggressors as victims. This book plans to challenge Western discourse on both globalization and terrorism by introducing the hopes, dreams, and aspirations of those who struggle for liberation from hegemony and injustice.

GLOBALIZATION

Regardless of national birth, our global reality is one of interdependence and shared destiny. We have been interconnected and interdependent from time immemorial. This global interdependence has been growing at a fast pace during the past century. Consequently, today we find ourselves inhabiting a world that has become a seamless and indivisible web of interconnected parts despite all the borders that divide its many states. The rapid pace of this interconnectedness has led scholars and opinion makers to label this phenomenon "globalization."

We entered the twenty-first century through the gates of globalization. Since then, globalization has become a powerful concept in almost all aspects of our lives. Governments so often blame their troubled economies on globalization. Corporations downsize in order to "compete" in the new global marketplace. Scholars debate globalization and its merits. Books and magazine articles carry the banner of globalization as their avenue to a broader market. But globalization is not just a recent phenomenon. The process of interdependence was also a process of globalization. What is new is the unprecedented pace of growth of globalization in the past decade. Prior to the fall of the Soviet Union, globalization was checked by the competition between East and West. After the demise of the Soviet Union, the challenge was left to a few weak, helpless nongovernmental organizations that have no chance to stop or even slow the momentum.

Globalization is the integration of markets, politics, values, and environmental concerns across the globe. This process of integration is driven by both the desire for higher profits and aspirations for greater economic prosperity or a better future for the planet and its inhabitants. Opponents of corporate globalization fear greater economic disparities between rich and poor, loss of cultural distinctiveness, or environmental degradation. Corporate managers see globalization as a means to develop new markets for their products and services. Governments often see globalization as their only viable course to avoid isolation and economic disaster if they oppose it or as a means to enhance their economic positions. Labor unions fear it because it diverts jobs away to distant places where cheap labor and sweatshops replace union work. Environmentalists fear the potentially unregulated production of goods for the sake of profit-producing environmental disasters. Investors in financial and stock markets support it as a means for portfolio growth. In sum, globalization is an extremely contentious topic.

Scholars are in the midst of this debate on globalization. Some equate globalization with interdependence, others with liberalization; others yet equate it with universalization, westernization, and even imperialism. Globalization has also been equated with transnationalization, but the reality is that the two concepts differ. Transnationalization enhances national entities, while globalization sometimes weakens them. Few scholars dismiss the utility of the concept altogether. Globalization, therefore, has become a concept causing unending controversy among scholars as it does in the media at large.

ROOT CAUSES AND CONSEQUENCES OF GLOBALIZATION

Religion, technology, economy, and empire are the engines that empower the drive toward globalization. Thus, power, wealth, and greed play a major role as root causes of globalization. Even the area of technology is arguably driven by the profit motive. In order to seriously discuss globalization, an analysis of the root causes and consequences is necessary.

Globalization is rooted in power and wealth. Whether for the glory of God, the empire, the nation, or the corporation, the spread of people, goods, and ideas grew and developed. In the process, hegemony continues into the twenty-first century under the guise of globalization. But the progression of hegemony has changed over time. In recent years, especially after the demise of the Soviet Union, the United States has found itself as the sole global hegemonic power. With its corporate wings reaching every part of the globe, the United States set out to protect its economic and military dominance. Recent trends in economic and political globalization under the auspices of the United States have contributed to greater deprivation and covered up many injustices. As multinationals move into a country, sweatshops often result, and dislocations in the traditional economy occur.

While globalization contributes to homogenization among peoples, economies, technologies, and cultures, it also has contributed to the concentration of power in one country or, at least, in a single ideological culture: the culture of liberalization, privatization, and marketization. This process of hegemonization is leading to the emergence and consolidation of a single hegemonic power.

Globalization has already increased the similarities among people everywhere. We now have global languages. English, French, Spanish, Chinese, and Arabic are, in essence, global as more than a billion people speak at least one of them. We also have a global economy. The world we live in is a web of economic interdependence where a downturn in one place has an impact on the rest of the world. Information has also gone global, as has education. All these forces point toward greater homogenization of our world. But when we look at the leaders of the homogenizing forces, we discover them to be predominantly Western. Therefore, homogenization is leading to hegemonization.

The most prominent and, to many, most disturbing aspect of hegemonization has been in the area of global homogenization. The imposition on the developing countries of what is called neoliberal economic reform through the World Bank, the World Trade Organization, and the International Monetary Fund has received most attention and caused serious concern. Such "reforms" include privatization, the dismantling of public welfare programs, and the shredding of the safety net for the poor. In many countries, such reforms have contributed to the reemergence of a huge gap between the rich and the poor. In Egypt, for example, the *infitah*, or liberalization, has led to a sizable rise in poverty along with a rise in the wealth of the few. The middle class is being squeezed out of existence. Naturally, those who refuse the tide of change will resist. Because of the preponderance of power, resistance takes on new forms. With the hegemonization of military power, the traditional forms of warfare are no longer possible. Therefore, new tools of resistance are being employed, including explosives, airplanes, missiles, chemicals, and information technologies.

GLOBALIZATION AS INTERDEPENDENCE

The most common usage of globalization usually has interdependence at its core. In fact, the world we inhabit has become seamless and indivisible despite the borders that divide its many states. Economically, the world is so interconnected that the livelihood of one depends on the work and production of many others. When we visit a nearby mall, we actually visit a global marketplace rather than a mere local shopping center. Whenever we buy Levis jeans made in Mexico and Hong Kong, Disney toys from Bangladesh, or Nikes from Vietnam and Indonesia, we are reaffirming the system of corporate globalization. Environmentally, the world we live in is an interdependent system where a malfunction of one part can lead to disasters throughout the system. Culturally, interdependence has increased with the growth in communication and technology.

It is with this background that scholars such as Paul Hirst and Grahame Thompson defined globalization in terms of "growing flows of trade and capital investment between countries."[1] Ali A. Mazrui also defined globalization in this strain as he explained that it "consists of processes which lead toward global interdependence and increasing rapidity of exchange across vast distances."[2] Scholars from the left and the right have reached similar conclusions. Thus, globalization means some form of interdependence.

GLOBALIZATION AS LIBERALIZATION

Many advocates of globalization argue that the fall of the Soviet Union ushered in a new era in international affairs. This new era of globalization represents the triumph of political and economic liberalization. Francis Fukuyama's "end of history" thesis views globalization as growth in free trade, civil society, and privatization of state-owned enterprises.[3] Similarly, Jagdish Bhagwati argues that globalization defined as capitalism is a system that "can destroy privilege and open up economic opportunity to many."[4] Such scholars see globalization as a way to remove trade restrictions, creating an open and "borderless" world economy and economic integration between First and Third World economies. In his book *The Lexus and the Olive Tree*, globalization proponent Thomas Friedman argues that "the spread of capitalism has raised living standards higher, faster and for more people than at any time in history. It has also brought more people into the middle class more quickly than at any time in human history."[5] Professor Deepak Lal of the University of California maintains that the "liberal international economic order promises unprecedented prosperity" as corporate globalization "expands current and future consumption possibilities by expanding the availability of foreign goods."[6]

Advocates of corporate globalization usually identify international economic institutions such as the International Monetary Fund (IMF), the World Bank, and the World Trade Organization (WTO) when describing the process of economic integration between the First and the Third World. These organizations work together to promote corporate expansion into and dominance of international markets. The WTO rules on trade disputes between member countries in an effort to reduce trade barriers or, according to many opponents of corporate globalization, to eliminate barriers to corporate profits. The IMF and World Bank provide loan packages to many Third World countries, accompanied by requirements that countries receiving loans lower their trade barriers and fulfill other requirements, such as the privatization of state industries and mandatory cuts in government workforces.

GLOBALIZATION AS UNIVERSALIZATION

Scholars, diplomats, and politicians often tell us that we live in a global village. Kofi Annan, former secretary-general of the United Nations, even went as far as to call for redefining sovereignty because of the forces of globalization.[7] With the rapid development of information technologies, such analysts foresee the advent of a planetary merger of cultures, ideas, and economics through a synthesis that will forge people all over the world into a closer unit. Stephen D. Krasner argues that the combined onslaught of monetary unions, the Internet, cable news, and nongovernmental organizations are challenging the notion of sovereignty even though they are not destroying it.[8] However, such a notion is up to dispute, considering that multinational corporations are still reliant on nation-states in order to exist as official institutions and, as government subsidies and protectionism suggest, in order to ensure their very survival. Corporations are also dependant on states to implement comprehensive trade agreements, such as the North American Free Trade Agreement (NAFTA) and the General Agreement on Tariffs and Trade (GATT), as well as to enforce the agendas of international business institutions, such as the IMF, World Bank, and WTO. In fact, one could easily argue that corporations are reliant on governments now more than ever.

GLOBALIZATION AS WESTERNIZATION

A number of scholars stress that globalization is leading to the spread of Western culture and practices around the world. Sports icons such as Kobe Bryant and Sammy Sosa, as well as pop stars such as Eminem and Britney Spears, have gained worldwide notoriety, the latter two performing shows throughout most of the world. In China, McDonald's restaurants expanded rapidly from 184 stores in 1997 to over 500 in 2002.[9] CNN International is now available throughout the world via television, the Internet, and instant text messaging. Be it McDonald's or CNN, the old ways of doing things are falling by the wayside and making room for the "modern" form of doing things. This process of "modernization" is tantamount to an Americanization of the globe.[10] Benjamin Barber argues that globalization is leading to a homogenized "McWorld" in which American popular culture and consumerism is overtaking the globe. Rejecting such American and consumerist domination, other cultures are producing movements of resistance, which Barber refers to as "jihad" (holy war).[11] Most resistance to globalization, however, comes from those who view globalization as corporate capitalism.

GLOBALIZATION AS CAPITALISM

Some scholars contend that globalization is an ideology of market economy. Manfred B. Steger refers to globalization as an ideology and calls it "globalism." In a superb study, Steger presents a sharp critique of this ideology of globalism as a new legitimation of capitalism on a global scale.[12] Perhaps this view is the most prominent outside the United States. European and Third World scholars often explain globalization in these critical terms. Martin Khor, for example, in an address to the International Forum on Globalization in New York City, proclaimed, "Globalization is what we in the Third World have for several centuries called colonization."[13] It is this view of globalization that is behind the motivation of those who wage the struggle to limit its negative impact.

This struggle has made globalization a focal point of hostile passions and occasional violent protests.

"ANTIGLOBALIZATION" FORCES

Many activists and critics of corporate power are often inaccurately labeled "antiglobalization protestors." To speak in such terms is far too vague—and even worse, it is inaccurate. When discussing globalization, it is necessary to distinguish between its various forms, including political, corporate (economic), military, environmental, technological, and cultural globalization. Take one specific example: environmentalists are usually in favor of expanding international environmental protections; hence, they support the globalization of environmental regulations and safeguards. On the other hand, they may be opposed to corporate globalization, specifically when corporations sacrifice environmental protections in pursuit of higher profits. Globalization may create new markets and wealth as it causes suffering, dislocations, and even violence. It is, however, both a source of repression and a catalyst for a struggle for social justice and human emancipation.

Critics of corporate globalization are many and growing in numbers. Some oppose this form of globalization because they see the share of the global income of the poorest people in the world dropping while Western corporate income continues to rise. The gap between the rich and the poor continues to widen, and the concerns of the poor seem to have been forgotten. While thousands die every day in Africa because of malnutrition, the number of millionaires in the United States grows at a steady pace. Take, for example, the case of a California billionaire who paid $2 million to clone his dog, Missy. As CNN reported the story on March 22, 2000, some poor fellow in some remote African village may question this decision as unsustainable and, perhaps, even obscene. The growing gap in wealth between the global North and the global South is a clear cause of concern for many opponents of globalization. One billion people—one-sixth of the population—now own up to 80 percent of the world's wealth, relegating the majority of the world's population into lives of poverty and desperation.[14]

Critics of corporate globalization condemn dominant business practices that prioritize profits to the exclusion of environmental, labor, and other social protections. Writer and activist William Greider argues that, as it exists today, "the global economy is running downhill, searching the world for the lowest common denominator in terms of national standards for wages, taxes, and corporate obligations to health, the environment, and stable communities."[15] Many opponents are quick to blame international financial and political institutions that contribute to the spread of corporate power. The WTO has been attacked for its string of one-sided, procorporate rulings. Lori Wallach and Michelle Sforza ridicule the WTO for its built-in bias that discourages democracy, pointing out that, "no democratically achieved environmental, health, food safety, or environmental law challenged at the WTO has survived attack. All have been declared barriers to trade."[16] Kevin Danaher, an activist and cofounder of the Global Exchanges, explains the trend of growing inequality throughout the world, claiming that "markets favor those with money, giving them opportunities to make even more money by taking it away from those with less wealth and less access to the rule-makers in government."[17] Danaher places much of the responsibility for this trend on international business institutions. The "overall thrust" of IMF and World Bank policies, for example, "is to keep workers and natural resources of the Third World open to exploitation by transnational corporations." Danaher equates such institutions with corporate neocolonialism, claiming that "they serve primarily as a control mechanism for First World elites to shape economic policy in Third World countries in such a way as to further the interests of transnational corporations and banks."[18]

AN INSTITUTIONAL CRITICISM OF THE IMF

Some of the strongest criticism of the neoliberal economic order has come from Greg Palast, investigative journalist for the *London Guardian* newspaper. In his book *The Best Democracy Money Can Buy*, Palast outlines many of the findings from his research concerning the practices of the IMF. Palast interviews former IMF chief economist Joseph Stiglitz, who discusses the conditions the IMF sets for every country receiving

World Bank loans. According to Stiglitz, every country is required by the IMF to enact the same four-step process.[19] Stiglitz and Palast are very critical of the requirements, which include the following:

1. *The mandatory privatization of state industries, such as electric and water companies.* Mandatory privatization is viewed as controversial, particularly when considering recent corporate failures such as Enron, not to mention the disastrous effects of such failures on national economies and peoples.

2. *Required "capital market liberalization,"* meaning the lowering of barriers restricting the flow of capital in and out of First and Third World states. Countries under economic crisis are extremely vulnerable in this case, as money usually flows out rather than in. Capital flight, in turn, further escalates economic meltdown.

3. *Ensured "market-based pricing,"* in other words, raising prices on essential goods and services. Many of these price increases deprive impoverished peoples of such necessities as water, electricity, and food. Logically, this trend has led to increased "social unrest,"[20] as the IMF unapologetically describes the problem. One example was seen in Ecuador in 2001 after the Ecuadorian government raised the price of cooking gas by 80 percent, inciting riots throughout the nation's capital. It was later shown that the IMF had masterminded the price increase and even predicted ahead of time that such an increase would likely provoke an Ecuadorian riot.[21]

4. *Compulsory free trade*, meaning required reductions in tariffs and other trade barriers flowing from the First World to the Third World. The catch, however, is that First World countries are allowed to continue with protectionism as usual, including legally protected monopolies under the WTO TRIPs agreement, massive subsidies for national industries, and continued tariffs that limit importation of foreign goods.

Even in rich countries, not everyone has benefited from corporate globalization. New corporate freedoms granted by globalization are leading to increased insecurity in the workplace. Between 1973 and

1997, it is estimated that the average income of the poorest 20 percent of Americans fell by 5 percent, while the average incomes of the richest 20 percent rose by over 40 percent—and the richest 5 percent rose by over 60 percent.[22] As manufacturers relocate to reap greater profits off cheaper labor in the global South, workers in the rich North are losing their source of livelihood. Manual laborers in particular are under threat as corporations shift their production to low-wage economies abroad. Implementation of NAFTA, for example, has resulted in the loss of 750,000 U.S. manufacturing jobs to Mexican maquiladoras (sweatshops).[23] American labor unions have suffered greatly as a result of NAFTA. Statistics show that throughout the 1990s, approximately half of union organizing in the United States had been disrupted as a result of employer threats to move company production from the United States to Mexican maquiladoras.[24]

As already mentioned, many workers in poor countries are not too thrilled with corporate globalization either. They are concerned about low wages and bad work environments. Sweatshops often generate wealth to corporate stockholders and perpetuate poverty for the workers. Some of the sweatshops employ child laborers working in unhealthy structures and dangerous environments.

Take, for example, the story of Iqbal Masih. Iqbal was one of the thousands of Pakistani children working in the "Oriental" carpet mills. Between 500,000 and 1,000,000 Pakistani children between the ages of four and fifteen work fourteen hours a day, six days a week, weaving carpets. Often, the children are chained to looms in carpet factories in Pakistan. These children are usually sent by their parents to work in the carpet factories to help support the family. They are often thin and malnourished. Their backs are usually curved because of the constant bending in front of the loom. Their hands are usually scarred, and they have difficulty breathing because of the constant inhaling of fabric dust. Under international pressure, Pakistan passed a law outlawing the practice of paying families for bonding their children in carpet labor. Consequently, a Pakistani human rights group, the Bonded Labor Liberation Front (BLLF), waged a campaign to free bonded children. Iqbal was one of those children freed after six years at the factory. His family had bonded him when he was four years old. Once freed, Iqbal became an active participant in the campaign to free other bonded children. He also traveled to Europe and the United States to expose the practice to consumers who buy the carpets. His personality and enthusiasm made him a very effective spokesperson on behalf of all bonded children in Pakistan. On April 16, 1995, a gunman shot thirteen-year-old Iqbal to death. While no conviction has been reached, it is clear that what the founder of the BLLF called the "carpet mafia" was responsible for his murder.

The story of Iqbal tells us that demand for "Oriental" carpets in rich countries contributes to bad production practices in poor ones. While the carpet manufacturers become wealthy, children suffer. Unless consumers are aware and are ready to boycott products produced by abusive means or take part in grassroots campaigns working against unfair labor practices, exploitation of the underprivileged will continue. Such exploitation is not limited to Pakistan or to carpet making but is widespread and can be found in all corners of the world.

Many environmentalists are opposed to corporate globalization as well. They fear that the interface between the new technologies, economic globalization, and centralized corporate power may lead to an unprecedented environmental trauma at a global scale. Environmentalists argue that corporations are disregarding the environment in the stampede for megaprofits and marketplace supremacy. The logic behind environmentalist campaigns rests on the principle that environmental protections must be pursued before ecological catastrophes become inevitable. Under this rationale, curbing emissions of carbon dioxide and developing renewable resources constitute essential steps in preventing global warming and environmental depletion. Furthermore, environmentalists advocate production of consumer goods that will meet the world's needs through environmentally sustainable methods. Environmental issues are receiving increased attention as trade across national borders grows and as people become more aware of how the degradation of the environment ultimately affects them. The introduction of genetically modified foods has been a strong rallying point for consumer advocates and environmentalists. The possible negative health consequences of genetically modified foods as indicated in early studies (as well as in the lack of many significant studies) has led many to criticize the corporate campaign of altering agricultural goods.[25]

Some intellectuals, activists, and religious groups oppose corporate globalization because of its impact on values. They see globalization as a new form of cultural imperialism. Lebanon's Party of God (Hizballah), for example, argues on its website that satellite TV spearheads the new assault of cultural imperialism along with the Internet, ensuring that "immorality" is just a click away. One can argue that cultural globalization is the most familiar form of globalization to the majority of people on earth. Almost everyone in the world knows the sports stars, the icons of popular culture, and the commercials for Coca-Cola. This was not the way it was fifty or so years ago. A few decades ago, most people lived in remote villages that had never seen a television, and people were amazed at the sounds of radio. Most people on earth were illiterate. Today, their grandchildren are on the move. They listen to music and watch television, and many participate in chat rooms and play games on the Internet. Clearly, the values of their parents or grandparents are not necessarily their own any more. This explosion of information may contribute to tensions and even violence.

The successes of other grassroots campaigns against corporate globalization have been supplemented with the recent actions of many Third World countries. For example, the deterioration of the 2003 WTO talks in Mexico, a direct result of the resistance of many leaders unhappy with the organization, has shown that, contrary to the dogma of Fukuyama and others, the spread of corporate capitalism throughout the world is not inevitable.[26]

GLOBALIZATION AND VIOLENCE

Any time the WTO, the World Bank, the IMF, or the leaders of the major economic powers meet, demonstrations break out. Some of these have turned violent. But the potential for violence related to globalization is much more serious and long lasting than occasional outbursts of some crowd. Violence against multinational corporate domination of markets is serious and has taken many shapes over the years. Corporate executives have been kidnapped and even murdered. Corporate outlets, such as McDonald's restaurants, have been attacked. Local police have arrested and killed many opponents of sweatshops or plantation work conditions. Guerrilla groups have also attacked multinational oil pipelines and disrupted the flow of oil to the market. Law enforcement agencies have strongly repressed nonviolent protests of organizations such as the WTO.[27] Such open and visible violence does occur, but other forms of violence may be taking place without much notice.

It is clear today that information crosses borders without consideration of territorial boundaries. Satellite transmissions need no visa. Governments are helpless here. If they try to stop the spread of information, they put their societies in danger of falling farther behind. If they allow it, they risk unwanted consequences. Take, for example, a remote village in Chad. People there still live a traditional way of life. They have no electricity, running water, or even a school in the village. Most adults are still illiterate. Imagine if one day the village elder returns from the city with a battery-operated television set along with a satellite dish. In the evening, as villagers gather to socialize and discuss their crops and livestock, the village elder now turns on the television set. Watching in amazement, the villagers may see an American, French, or Italian movie or some show produced in California, New York, London, or Paris. At that time, a new and strange world begins to unfold in front of the villagers' eyes. They see kitchens with faucets that bring water indoors, switches that turn darkness into light, cars, streets, indoor plumbing, and a way of life they never imagined could exist. A couple of hours later, the village elder turns the set off, and villagers depart to their mud or clay homes to sleep on their dirt floors. As they sleep, they are now likely to have new kinds of dreams. No more are they dreaming about rain, milking the cows, or harvesting the crops. Instead, they are likely to dream of having an amazing faucet that brings water inside a home or of having a car or electricity. Once this happens, it starts a process of "migration of dreams." The dissemination of information contributes to new dreams among the poor. The wealthy and advanced countries are, in essence, encroaching on the dreams of the poor.

The process of migration of dreams is a common occurrence. It takes place all the time and in all places. In rich countries, when people see a television program in a beautiful setting, they too may dream about going to that place someday. An old television show called *The Love Boat*, set on a cruise ship, contributed to a huge growth in the cruise industry. The idea of a commercial is often an attempt at creating the intentional migration of dreams. If we now go back to the village in Chad, we find that as the villagers begin to have greater dreams for themselves and their families, their level of expectation grows. Consequently, the villagers may now expect running water, roads, and even cars. The government is so poor that it cannot afford to provide running water or electricity or roads to every small village. It may have greater priorities of providing such infrastructures to major cities where large numbers of people reside. Or, possibly, the government may prefer to put its limited resources into health care and education rather than building roads to such a remote place with very few occupants.

Social scientists have identified the gap between expectations and achievement as a major contributor to violence. This theory is known as "relative deprivation." Ted Robert Gurr defines relative deprivation as the gap between what one gets and what one believes he or she should get. Gurr tells us that the larger the gap between the two, the more likely an individual is to turn to violence.[28] If this respected and popular theory is accurate, then it is fair to say that the rising expectations of the poor in the Chadian village or elsewhere could contribute to increasing violence. That violence may be directed against children, a spouse, neighbors, or even the authority as represented by government. If some rebel group comes to the village to recruit fighters against the government, one could argue that more villagers are now likely to join because of the increased gap between expectations and achievement. The globalization of information dissemination, therefore, may contribute to violence.

The increasing pace of change with globalization in itself may also contribute to violence. When societies go through a fast pace of change, they often experience polarization. Some people support the change, while others oppose it. At times, the division between the two groups is so great that they clash, and a civil war erupts. In the United States, when the country underwent a major transformation from an agricultural economy based on the plantation and slavery as its major means of production into an industrial society dependent on coal and labor, the country slipped into a civil war. A similar phenomenon took place in England during the Cromwell revolution, in France in 1789, and in Russia in the early part of the twentieth century. Today, with the rapid pace of global change, one could argue that our global community could be entering into a phase of a global civil war. Those who oppose the change may have already begun their struggle to secede from the globalized union. Terror may be their weapon. After all, the concept of terrorism was coined during the French Revolution's Reign of Terror.

TERRORISM

History is often written not by heroes but by those who execute them. Current history is written in a similar manner. Therefore, the terrorist and the victim of terror are often confused. Victims are often called terrorists, and those who terrorize others are frequently portrayed as victims of terror. The confusion occurs because of the lack of a clear delineation of what terrorism is. As a concept, terrorism has acquired an extraordinary status in American public discourse. There is no doubt today that terrorism has replaced Communism as the leading enemy of the United States. Lacking a clear definition acceptable by all parties, terrorism remains in the eye of the beholder. A terrorist is such to his or her enemies and a freedom fighter to his or her supporters.

Terrorism is difficult to define because it is inherently political. While many people could identify terrorist acts when they hear of them, the fact remains that most people lack a precise definition of the concept. Many would never think of acts done on their own or government's behalf to be terrorist. The terrorist, somehow, is always the other. There are many ironies when it comes to pointing out "the terrorist." When Israeli leaders refer to Palestinian ones as terrorist, one cannot help but remember that British colonists called some of those same Israeli leaders "terrorist" when Britain ruled Palestine as a mandate territory. Is terrorism ever accepted and justified? The answer seems to be obvious: whenever terrorism is justified, those who feel that it is just do not call it terrorism. Instead, a host of other concepts are used, including fight for independence, liberation, struggle, jihad, self-defense, or revolution.

DEFINITION OF TERRORISM

Terrorism is one of those concepts that make wonderful political tools. Politicians around the world use it to describe their armed opponents. Colonial powers used it to refer to nationalist groups fighting them for independence. Many Third World countries identify First World aggression with terrorism. In the aftermath of September 11, 2001, the United States became involved in a War on Terror. This war took U.S. troops to Afghanistan and a number of other countries and led to the reorganization of its security and intelligence apparatus. It is clear today that our world is pregnant with change. The phenomenon that is called terrorism has ushered in a new era for world politics. The future is not easy to predict. Scholars, however, are always ready to read their crystal balls to tell us about future developments. Some spoke of an "American Century," while others discussed a "Clash of Civilizations." A number of commentators have pointed to September 11, 2001, as the confirmation of the predicted clash with other civilizations. But the fact remains that terrorism is not the monopoly of a single civilization. We cannot afford to continue to succumb to myths. Change is constant, and its causes are often similar. Its direction is less predictable. The myth of the wild-eyed terrorist who is taught to kill Israelis, Europeans, or Americans from birth must be dropped in favor of reality. Those who carry out so-called terrorist activities are often people in despair whose lives have been tormented by those who are more powerful than they are. Terrorism is not genetic, nor is it a disease. Those who engage in it come in all colors and from all cultures. Terrorism is a symptom rather than a disease. It has other causes. Most definitions of the concept, however, seem to focus on the symptom and avoid any reference to its causes. Terrorism itself, regardless of definition, is a dynamic and rapidly changing phenomenon.

A dictionary for diplomats defines terrorism as the "use of violence against non-combatants, civilians or other persons normally considered to be illegitimate targets of military action for the purpose of attracting attention to a political cause, forcing those aloof from the struggle to join it, or intimidating opponents into concessions."[29] David J. Whittacker lists a number of definitions of terrorism in his reader on the subject. They include the following:

- The unlawful use of force or violence against persons or property to intimidate or coerce a government, a civilian population, or any segment thereof, in furtherance of political or social objectives (FBI).
- The calculated use of violence or threat of violence to inculcate fear, intended to coerce or intimidate governments or societies as

to the pursuit of goals that are generally political, religious or ideological (U.S. Department of Defense).

- Premeditated, politically motivated violence perpetuated against noncombatant targets by sub-national groups or clandestine agents, usually intended to influence an audience (U.S. Department of State).[30]

The current Israeli prime minister, Benjamin Netanyahu, defines terrorism as "the deliberate and systematic assault on civilians to inspire fear for political ends."[31] In order to create such fear, terrorist attacks against individuals, groups, and states must appear to be random. The uncertainty concerning potential terrorist attacks is what makes terrorism so dangerous, as the example of the Washington, D.C., sniper attacks of 2002 demonstrates. No one knows who may be the next target or when or where they may be attacked.

Most scholars seem to agree that terrorism is a value-laden concept. Many of them view terrorism as a political label rather than a meaningful research concept. When individuals call others terrorist, they are, in effect, prescribing some moral connotation because that term implies irrationality, fanaticism, and violence. To some activist in what the U.S. government may call a terrorist group, the group may represent liberation, freedom, self-defense, righteousness, virtue, or justice. Given this confusion, terrorism remains contested as a concept.

For the purposes of this book, terrorism is defined as a political label given to people who are perceived to be planning or carrying out acts of violence for political objectives. The violence may be directed against individuals and sometimes property. The violence may not always be that of individuals or groups. A government's armed forces may be labeled terrorist, as they often are, by the party at the receiving end of that violence. Such a definition of the concept of terrorism clearly takes it out of the realm of "objective" scholarship and places it in a complex political context. Social scientists are not lacking in concepts on violence, assassinations, bombings, hijackings, or others sorts of attacks that politicians often label as terrorism. The label of terrorism, when applied across the board, often leads to the disfiguring of genuine causes of liberation. Politicians often manage to advance the issue of terrorism in a reversed form to the forefront of public discourse. Thus, the Palestinians—uprooted, denied their basic national and human rights, rendered refugees for decades, and constantly exposed to state terror—are collectively labeled by the desperate acts of the few in their midst. On the other hand, the initiators of the terror of occupation, land confiscation, curfews, and other illegal restrictions on the lives of the Palestinians are collectively perceived as the victims of terror. Similarly, when South Africans were struggling against the terror of apartheid, they were collectively labeled terrorists by the minority regime, while the oppressive forces of the government were perceived as the victims of terrorism. In Northern Ireland and in many other places around the world, similar analogies are to be found.

The globalization of violent conflicts has led to unprecedented levels of human suffering. Terrorism has constituted a necessary component in such conflicts. While the migration of dreams stems from cultural and technological globalization, a different process called the migration of nightmares is a direct result of global violence and terrorism. As history has shown, the terrorism of empires as well as regional powers has been the main force driving this phenomenon. The powerful often terrorize the weak and bring nightmares into the lives of the helpless. On occasion, the weak and oppressed carry their struggle into the heartland of their oppressors, bringing nightmares to those who live there. Just as dreams migrate across the globe, nightmares do as well. This cycle of "migration of dreams and nightmares" has become part of our lives in this era of globalization.

RELEVANCE OF GLOBALIZATION AND TERRORISM IN THE TWENTY-FIRST CENTURY

Our planet entered the twenty-first century through the gates of violence and proceeded into the chambers of economic hardships. The assault on the United States on September 11, 2001, marked the start of a bloody conflict between the United States and some "invisible" groups and individuals. The attacks themselves targeted symbolic structures. Their impact, however, was very real. Almost 3,000 innocent civilians died on that day alone. A whole economy was set back, and the psyche of a nation was tormented. The World Trade Center buildings symbolized global capitalism under American leadership. The Pentagon symbolized American power and its global reach. Aside from the innocent victims, what was attacked on that day represented the dominance of the United States in a globalized world. But the real victims of that violence were people who were going about their lives, those trying to raise a family and build a future. The terror of that day lingers on. While the targets may have had political significance, the victims were innocent and nonpolitical.

It became clear on that day that even Americans must pay attention. They too are targets of outrageous violence. Perhaps most of the innocent people who perished that day had never heard of al Qaeda or Osama bin Laden, and most probably could not point to Afghanistan on a map. Not any more. Americans today learned a lot more about peoples, groups, and countries that are different and distant. The rest of the world, on the other hand, always knew about the United States. They had to deal with its products, its military, or its foreign policies, all of which impact their daily lives. The interdependent world we live in has made us all uneasy neighbors where the behavior of one state, group, or individual can have serious ramifications for the lives of others in seemingly distant places.

September 11, 2001, is likely to go down in the annals of terrorism as a defining moment. The atrocities of that day were condemned throughout the world as crimes against humanity. There was a near global unanimity that all countries must act together to rid the world of individuals and groups that carry out such atrocities. But the U.S. response was more unilateral and resembled the politics of the previous century. The massive bombing of Afghanistan and President Bush's rhetoric of "good versus evil" were reminders of times past where the global division between East and West somehow justified acts of violence in the name of wiping out Communism or evil. The fact remains that we live in an age of globalization with the United States as the global leader. Our world today is similar to a ship on the high seas. On this global ship, there are people who live in first-class cabins, others in second, some in third, and many way at the bottom in fourth-class cabins. Regardless of where we live, we need to be concerned about the well-being of those in the lower cabins. If we allow those cabins to rot, rust, and leak, the whole ship will sink. We in the United States of America do not wish to live in first-class cabins. We want to live in the captain's cabin. We want to be number one and second to none. While the captain of the ship has the luxury of the captain's cabin, the captain also has responsibility for the well-being of the whole ship. Many Americans want to be the captain of the ship, but they prefer not to take responsibility for the state of the global ship. We cannot have it both ways. Either we lead, or we get out of the way.

Leadership in this era of globalization must apply international law blindly to all parties on board. A leader cannot hope to succeed without uniform application of the law. The United States is itself a subject of international law. Its friends and allies are subjects as well. Yet U.S. foreign policy continues to be selective in its application of law. For example, when Iraq invaded Kuwait in violation of international law, the United States rushed to correct that wrong. But when Israel occupied Arab lands in violation of the same clauses of international law, the United States dragged its feet and continues to do so. The American response to Iraq's attacks on Kuwait's sovereignty appeared especially hypocritical when considering that the United States was condemned by the United Nations earlier for its own act of unlawful aggression with the invasion of Panama. Those on the other side find it hard to respect this type of selectivity. As they fall into despair, some of them might carry out acts of outrageous violence that many will call terrorism. This analysis is not to condone such acts but to help better understand from where they originate. In this age of globalization, the world needs consistent and principled leadership rather than a parochial one. Ironically, as globalization proceeds at a fast pace, the threat of terrorism unites people within nation-states in parochial and more nationalist ways. The attacks of September 11, 2001, for example, led to almost unprecedented national unity among Americans and a new fervor of patriotism unseen in decades. Today our world is moving in both directions at the same time. In the meantime, our global ship keeps drifting in an aimless fashion toward a future that prohibits any serious efforts at prediction.

Globalization has had consequences on values and ethics as it does on economics. Terrorism has also had consequences on values and economics. Both impact the way we think and live. Together they have ushered in a new era of international and global relations. No country can afford to fashion its policies on old norms. In our modern world, no nation-state is fully sovereign anymore. Individuals and groups dedicated to challenging the global system through unabashed violence can and have disrupted normal global interactions. The real human cost of globalization is serious, just as the real and psychological impact of terrorism is. The new circumstances call for new thinking that adapts globalization to legal and ethical standards and the search for national and global security to moral restraints. We cannot afford to fight "evil" by committing evil. Our menacing adversaries are concealed in nonstate networks that feed on resentment, double standards, and arrogance. If we hope to create a more peaceful world, we all must act as part of the global community that is working to bring security through legal means in a collective manner with all other states in the world. In order to achieve peace and security, we must strive to achieve justice for all. The recent fiscal and economic meltdown is likely to enhance conflict rather than contain it. Justice becomes less possible when the world is suffering its very first global recession.

THE GREAT GLOBAL RECESSION
AND GLOBALIZATION

Recessions are not new to capitalist economies. What is new in the recession of 2008–2009 is the global reach of the economic downturn. In fact, one could argue that this event was the first ever truly global recession. In late 2008, the global financial system experienced a serious crisis unmatched in history. Major financial institutions collapsed and global stock markets fell drastically. The new wave of capitalism on a global scale, what Manfred Steger calls "globalism," has shown its ugly face. The West's economic troubles have migrated to cover the planet. Naturally, the most severely affected are always the poorest of the poor. Developing countries felt the downturn in real terms. The twenty-year trend of decreasing abject poverty was halted. The World Bank reported an increase in the poverty rate of 1.5 percent in urban parts of East Asia, South Asia, the Middle East, and sub-Saharan Africa by the end of 2008.[32]

The astronomical growth in the wealth and influence of multinational corporations over the past few decades has finally come home to roost. Financial institutions had to be bailed out by governments. Large industries begged for loans from governments, and global corporations required government assistance. Suddenly the free market is not free after all.

CHAPTER 2

TERRORISM AND ITS ROOT CAUSES

Many people see globalization and terrorism as recent phenomena. The fact is neither globalization nor terrorism is new. Globalization did not start with the fall of the Soviet Union, and terrorism did not begin with the September 11, 2001, events. Both have deep roots that reach far into history. Both are important and retain multiple meanings, causes, and consequences. This chapter provides the conceptual and historical background of both. While recent trends in economic, cultural, and political globalization have contributed to greater deprivation and violence, both globalization and terrorism have been ongoing long before recent days.

It is imperative to identify the root causes of terrorism, whether individuals, organizations, or nation-states commit the acts. What is clear after hundreds of years is that terrorism is not a genetic disease but a societal one. Terrorist acts are not merely the acts of fanatics but are committed for clear purposes and by people with clear agendas. Terrorism may be traced back to two fundamental, underlying motivations: the struggle for power and domination and acts of desperation in response to this power struggle. The migration of dreams and nightmares bear a special relationship with the proliferation of terrorism.

GLOBALIZATION AND TERRORISM IN HISTORY

When did globalization and terrorism start? This question has contributed to a major debate among scholars. The fact is both globalization and terrorism have no specific point of origin. Both have been ongoing in some fashion throughout time. While the words *globalization* and *terrorism* are both quite new, their practice and processes are rather old.

THE RISE AND DEVELOPMENT OF GLOBALIZATION

Professor Ali A. Mazrui suggests that four forces have been major engines behind globalization over the years. He cites religion, technology, economy, and empire as the forces that have reinforced the process of globalization.[1] Jan Aart Scholte provides a long chart chronicling what he calls incipient globalization, starting with the first world's fair in 1851.[2] Others, such as Immanuel Wallerstein, argue that globalization dates back to the rise of the modern capitalist economy.[3] It is obvious that scholars do not agree on a specific starting point for globalization. Depending on how one defines the concept, various trends would emerge as to when globalization emerged. Given that our definition in this book did not limit globalization to a specific sphere, such as the economy, we could argue that a variety of processes reinforcing each other have worked to globalize our planet over time. Take, for example, the globalizing impact of the rise of empires in relation to the spread of religion. Christianity developed in Palestine and spread to other continents, and it globalized value systems across many regions of the world. Of course, religion and empire coincided as Emperor Constantine I of Rome decided to tolerate Christianity in A.D. 313 as they did with explorations and colonialism. Religion and empire also coincided with the rise and growth of Islam. Islam grew as a result not of converting a ready-made empire but of building a new one. The rise of Buddhism from Hindu culture was also a globalizing phenomenon. Buddhism spread outside of India and became a dominant belief system throughout East and Southeast Asia.

Trade also acted as a force for globalization. Trade for silk, for example, created the Silk Road, which connected China to many distant places. Trade for cotton, tea, and spices contributed to explorations that brought the Americas into the global system through colonialism and settlement. Trade, economy, and empire were major motives for explorations and colonialism. As the colonists arrived at new destinations, they imposed their own systems of governance, economic activity, and religion on the native populations or those who survived the advent of the colonial process.

The wave of colonialism came on the heels of the Industrial Revolution, which mated technology and economics and resulted in dramatic advancement in productivity and a leap forward in the greed of those who managed it. The consequences were large empires and great oppression. The new empires became truly global, and the suffering of those on the receiving end became permanent.

Colonialism represented perhaps the cruelest amalgamation of globalization and terrorism as millions of people perished under the guns of the colonists. What some now label the American genocide, committed by colonists and the American government against Native American peoples, constituted one of many instances where the lust for colonial power subordinated the rights of indigenous populations.[4] Those spared from murder were forced into a system of slavery and sent to faraway lands. Brutal conditions defined the transportation of African slaves to the North American colonies. Slaves were packed into small areas during their transport, often leading to their suffocation. All told, the brutality of the slave trade led to the deaths of one in three Africans during their trips to North America.[5] The slave trade and the assault on indigenous tribes in the Americas are a few examples of the migration of nightmares. Terrorist acts committed by the American military against hundreds of Native American women and children at massacres such as Sand Creek[6] and Wounded Knee[7] would forever haunt those who survived such atrocities. Children witnessed the murder of their parents; women forever lost their husbands, children, brothers, fathers, and grandparents to the onslaught of the American military.[8]

During the twentieth century, many wars of national liberation took place in a global trend of independence. Two world wars occurred. Warfare, in effect, became globalized. Wars of national liberation were influenced by global ideals of self-determination and freedom and were enhanced by a global network of support. Whether in Algeria, Vietnam, or South Africa, the struggle of the locals was supported by a wide global network including people from the ruling societies. The world wars were also a manifestation of globalization. Power rivalries became global in both wars as they did in the following Cold War. The globalization of so many wars has been accompanied by a significant question: are acts of war, such as attacks on civilian populations, considered terrorism? While the universal application of the terrorism-war interpretation is bound to incite intense controversy inside as well as outside of intellectual circles, it raises interesting implications for global superpowers. Instead of exclusively labeling the acts of losers as terrorism, such as those of Germany, Italy, and Japan during World War II, the question is now turned to the winners who write the history books. Would, for example, Allied fire bombings of Tokyo and Dresden during World War II or, as some dissidents imply from their critiques, the nuclear bombings of Hiroshima and Nagasaki qualify not only as acts of war but also acts of terrorism?[9] If this contention were taken seriously, it would substantiate the theory that terrorist acts include those committed by states struggling for power and domination. Acceptance of this argument may also serve to limit the military activities abroad of superpowers such as the United States.

With the end of the Cold War, a new gap emerged between the newly independent societies' need for social transformation and the U.S. insistence on stability. People who became independent during the past century are longing for change while the United States is obsessed with global power and order. As the gap widened between the expectations of those who want change and the contentment of the United States, a new type of global confrontation began to emerge. The antagonistic relationship turned bloody on few occasions. One of those took place on September 11. This current historical stage started as the Industrial Revolution merged with the new information revolution. This contributed to the rising expectations and new aspirations the world over. It also contributed to a reinforcement of First World dominance in technology and economy. The United States used that advantage to create its empire through Americanization at the widest possible global scale. The engine of the new globalization more than ever before rests on capital formation and profit making.

THE RISE AND DEVELOPMENT OF TERRORISM

The word *terrorism* dates back to the French Revolution. It was first used in 1794 to refer to the use of terror by governments against their own people. The Reign of Terror was a stage in the French Revolution. But the use of violence against innocents for political purposes can be traced back to the earliest days of "civilization." The Bible itself is full of references to the use of violence in an unjust manner. The pharaohs of Egypt are said to have used such forms of violence against the old Hebrews. Samson brought down the temple on himself and his enemies, many of whom were innocent spectators, long before modern suicide bombers tried. Pirates took over ships for gain in wealth and power long before hijackers of planes were conceived. Stories of troops or rebels burning villages and killing its innocent inhabitants are as old as human history itself. Most prevalent throughout history, though, has been terrorism committed in the imperial effort for world domination. For the purposes of this book, however, we divide the history of terrorism into three phases: premodern, early modern, and current.

The premodern phase includes all recorded history up to the end of the eighteenth century. While this is a broad categorization, it refers essentially to the times before guns, explosives, and hijackings. During such times, terrorism revolved around assassinations and murders. The Zealots of the Holy Land, the Hashashin of the Middle East, and ancient Rome and Greece practiced assassinations at different times. This practice continued in subsequent eras and societies as well. Of course, assassinations still take place. The uniqueness of this stage is that the victim of murder or assassination was normally alleged to be guilty of some wrongdoing. In other words, there existed a moral justification for assassination. Statues were even erected to honor assassins. Old Greeks built a statue to honor such assassins as Harmodias and Aristogeiton. Modern-day assassinations seem to lack such justification.

To speak accurately of terrorism during this period, it is necessary to include early imperialism. An accurate starting point could include the acts of the Greeks, including their sieges on foreign cities such as Herodotus and Troy. The aggression and oppression committed by Alexander the Great in his conquests of what is today the Middle East also served as an important early model for future empires. The Punic Wars between Rome and Carthage saw the laying of siege to and the sacking of cities as a main imperial strategy. The fall of the Western Roman Empire in A.D. 476 as well as the Ottoman Turks' sacking of the Eastern Roman Empire (Byzantium) at Constantinople in A.D. 1456 demonstrated the early viciousness of terrorist attacks against civilian populations.

The early modern phase includes the nineteenth and early twentieth centuries up to just before World War I. This phase included violence by nationalists and other extremists accompanied by spectacular assassinations. The Paris Commune, the Haymarket bombing of 1886 in Chicago (although it was never determined who was responsible), and men such as Ravachol setting off explosions are examples of anarchist terror during this phase. Irish and Armenian nationalists exemplified terrorism of that era. The two most significant assassinations were those of Czar Alexander II in 1881 and Archduke Ferdinand of Austro-Hungary in 1914. It was the latter assassination that precipitated World War I.

Despite the harshness of these individual terrorist acts, they pale in comparison to acts of state terror in this period. The brutality of the mass murder and displacement of Native American tribes by European colonialists, while clearly terrorist in nature, was carried out under the justification of Manifest Destiny. Extremely brutal as well was the genocide committed against over a million Armenians by the Ottoman Empire during the late nineteenth and early twentieth centuries. The early modern period was marked predominantly by the conflict of European empires, including the French, British, Spanish, and German. The British Empire expanded its reach as far as China, which was forcibly opened to the Western drug trade after the end of the Opium Wars and China's signing of the Treaty of Nanking in 1842. The full extent of Britain's globalization of terror emerged during this conflict. As a major drug trafficker, Great Britain produced much of its opium in its colony of India, forcing opium shipments into China through the East India Company. The Opium Wars resulted in the deaths of thousands of Chinese as the British systematically destroyed houses, towns, and communities along the Chinese coast; the conflict also left the Chinese with the problems accompanying the explosion in drug use and addiction. The European colonization of Africa and exploitation of its resources stands as one of the largest globalized terrorist acts in history. Belgian King Leopold II seized the territory now known as the Congo (then the Belgian Congo) in the late nineteenth century; his forces committed massacres, burned villages, and enslaved the region's inhabitants.[10] Historian Adam Hochschild called Leopold's acts mass murder "of genocidal proportions."[11] Mass murder committed by the European powers was accompanied by the rape of African natural resources and the persistence of the global slave trade. German atrocities in southwestern Africa in the early twentieth century consisted of the attempted extermination of the Herero and Nama peoples. The Boer War of 1899 was fought between the British and the South African Republic (Transvaal) and the Orange Free State. Farms were burned, crops were destroyed, and thousands of Boer women and children were forced into concentration camps, resulting in the deaths of thousands.

The modern phase, which is most relevant to our lives today, deserves the most study. The period stretches from World War I to the present. This phase included group struggles for national independence and the waging of warfare against dominant powers (often insurgency movements). The Zionist movement in Palestine waged such a struggle against the British and the local Palestinian population in order to create their own independent Jewish state. In Algeria, Kenya, Cyprus, South Yemen, and many other places, similar struggles were carried out in order to achieve independence. In some instances, the struggle was waged beyond the borders of the subject territory. Forms of terrorism, such as the hijacking of planes and bombings of specific targets, became more common during the modern phase. This phase also included ideological and religious groups that engaged in the destruction and murder of innocent civilians for political objectives. Groups such as the Weathermen in the United States, the Red Brigades in Italy, and the Japanese Red Army carried out such attacks in wealthy capitalist states. Religion-based groups such as al Qaeda carried out even more outrageous attacks and continue to exist and even grow. Other Islamist groups are becoming more active all the time. The recent attacks in Mumbai, India, represent a case in point. Similarly, Jewish extremist groups are becoming bolder as are Buddhist and Hindu groups. Christians in Nigeria and other places are also carrying out violent attacks more regularly. Somali pirates in the Gulf of Aden are indiscriminate as they attack ships belonging to corporations and states of all faiths.

Government-sanctioned terrorism in the modern period merits significant discussion. World War I provided one of the most ugly examples of the horrors of twentieth-century warfare. It is estimated that as many as nine million peopled died from the war, one and a half million in the first battle of Marne alone.[12] The period of World War I saw the rise of the machine gun as well as chemical weapons, both of which would play important roles in terrorist acts in the following decades. Despite the enormous casualties of World War I, it took until World War II for the full extent of terrorist warfare to materialize. As discussed earlier, the Holocaust, followed by the Allied firebombings of Dresden and Tokyo and the nuclear bombings of Hiroshima and Nagasaki, represented some of the most severe effects of terrorism directed at civilian populations.

The Holocaust resulted in the deaths of over six million Jews and five million Polish, gypsies, homosexuals, and other "undesirables." This act symbolized the ultimate horror of which humankind is capable. Probably equally vicious were the crimes of Stalin, whose reign of terror ended in the murder of an estimated seven to ten million Ukrainians (who died under his forced starvation) and maybe as many as twenty to twenty-five million throughout the entire Soviet Empire. What seems most disturbing about Stalin's atrocities is the fact that 50 percent of Russians today look at Stalin as a positive historical figure.[13] Such fanciful conceptions reinforce the extraordinary influence and power of state propaganda. Most often ignored in the history of terrorism during World War II are the American nuclear bombings of Hiroshima and Nagasaki. The bombing of Hiroshima resulted in the deaths of around 140,000 people and that of Nagasaki around 70,000.[14] Eyewitness accounts of the Hiroshima bombing are as depressing as they are disturbing. John Hersey, author of *Hiroshima*, describes the despair evident during the first night after the bombing: "By nightfall, ten thousand victims of the explosion had invaded the Red Cross Hospital."[15] Describing the scene within the hospital, Hersey explains, "Ceilings and partitions had fallen; plaster, dust, blood, and vomit were everywhere. Patients were dying by the hundreds, but there was nobody to carry away the corpses. Some of the hospital staff distributed biscuits and rice balls, but the charred-house smell was so strong that few were hungry. . . . Thousands of patients and hundreds of dead were in the yard and on the driveway."[16]

The Cold War represented the extreme measures that Soviet and American leaders were willing to take in order to achieve global power. The American attack on Indochina resulted in the deaths of millions of Vietnamese, Laotian, and Cambodian peasants. Spraying of chemical defoliants over rural areas led to negative health effects for many of the Vietnamese people, at the same time causing substantial environmental damage.[17] Possibly the most disturbing acts were massacres such as My Lai, where American soldiers executed Vietnamese women and children.[18] The Soviet invasion of Afghanistan in 1979 also resulted in numerous atrocities. Bombing campaigns destroyed entire towns, leaving thousands dead or homeless. One of the most disturbing genocides in the Cold War period occurred in Cambodia. The Communist Khmer Rouge regime, led by Pol Pot, sought to remove any foreign influence from his country, no matter how slight. Pol Pot's campaign led to the internal displacement of millions of Cambodians and the eventual murder of over a million people.[19] Equally appalling was the Indonesian genocide committed against the residents of the small island of East Timor. The genocide was made possible by American military and economic support for the corrupt Suharto dictatorship and by support by the Central Intelligence Agency (CIA) for Suharto's overthrow of former President Ahmed Sukarno.[20] Some estimates indicate that the Indonesian government murdered as many as 200,000 people, or up to a third of the preinvasion population.[21]

Genocide, or the mass killing of innocent people, has been going on for a long time. The genocide in Rwanda in 1994 took the lives of 800,000 innocent people and was carried out by ethnic gangs and extremists. The Hutu extremists, without opposition from the global community, carried out horrific acts of violence against a helpless Tutsi population. Similar acts of violence against innocent people are still going on in the Darfur region of Sudan. Terrorizing innocent people, therefore, can take many shapes and can be carried out not only by a few fanatics making their plans in caves or hideouts, but also by leaders issuing orders from the presidential or royal compounds.

SEPTEMBER 11 AND THE GROWTH
OF GLOBAL TERRORISM

It is possible that future historians may point to the attacks of September 11 as the start of a new phase in terrorism. If al Qaeda and other similar groups survive and continue their deadly attacks, some future historian may argue that a new phase of more deadly and mostly theologically based terror began. Religious zealotry has been a major source of terrorism for a long time. It is global and not limited to a specific religion, even though emphasis in the United States has been placed on Islamic groups. Christian, Jewish, Hindu, Buddhist, and Sikh terrorism has taken place in many parts of the world. When a Jewish settler shoots worshippers in a mosque in Hebron, a Hindu burns down a mosque in India, a Sikh assassinates a prime minister, or a Christian brings down a building in Oklahoma City killing scores of innocents, terror occurs. Yet attention in the United States is unifocal, focusing on the Islamic variety. This is what the late Eqbal Ahmed called a parcelized approach to terror.[22]

Recent terrorist attacks have taken a toll on old theories of international relations. No more can we only speak of nation-states as the main actors in the global arena. Attacks like those of September 11, 2001, in the United States and December 2008 in Mumbai, India, have clearly shown the instant impact of nonstate actors on international relations. In fact, the state has not always been the predominant actor in global politics nor has it ever been the sole one. After all, the state-centric model of international politics dates back only to the 1648 Peace of Westphalia. The past few decades have witnessed a rapid increase in the number and significance of nonstate actors. Multinational corporations have grown in power to be able to put the brakes on the power and authority of national leaders. The 2008–2009 financial crises have proven the power of private corporations. Similarly, independent groups such as al Qaeda, Somali pirates, Kashmiri Islamists, or Spanish separatists have a marked effect on domestic and international political behavior.

CRITICISMS OF THE WAR ON TERROR

Both the Afghanistan and Iraq wars will be discussed in a later chapter. A few words here on how such wars may have enhanced terrorism rather than minimize it, are in order. While the Bush administration's War on Terror found support in the United States in its first year, it has fallen under an incredible amount of controversy throughout the world, whether it be in "rogue states" or among American allies. Some will argue that the war in Iraq contributed to the downfall of the Republican Party in the United States and, perhaps, to the global financial downturn of 2008–2009. Justifications for the wars against Afghanistan and Iraq have been prevalent in the American mass media and in mainstream political discourse; criticisms were not. It is under this reality, then, that it is important to summarize and analyze criticisms of the War on Terror.

Many critics of the war against Afghanistan argue that, rather than reducing the terrorist threat to the United States, the deaths of Afghan civilians from American and allied bombs have actually increased the terrorist threat. It is clear that such deaths only hurt any meaningful efforts at fighting terror, as it is impossible to fight terror by participating in it. The deaths of innocent Afghans and Iraqis by American forces may very well have increased the number of people throughout the world that view the United States as the primary threat to world peace and justice.

An even larger concern than the over 3,000 Afghan civilians who died in the initial two weeks from American bombing[23] was the possibility that American bombing, after disrupting humanitarian relief (food shipments) efforts, led to the suffering of millions of Afghans. The United Nations estimated that by the time of the U.S. bombing, up to five and a half million Afghans would be reliant on UN humanitarian relief, specifically food, in order to survive.[24] Furthermore, many international food relief agencies pleaded with the United States to stop the bombing in order for aid to be delivered safely to those in dire need. The *Sunday Times* of London estimated that up to seven million Afghans were in "dire need of humanitarian relief" at the start of the bombing.[25] American food drops were at nowhere near the level needed to feed millions. Throughout October 2001, for example, the United States on average dropped about 37,500 food packages a day. In the best-case scenario, all packages being received would mean that just over 1 percent of those in need were accounted for; in the worst case (depending on the number of people in need), just over one-half of 1 percent of those in need were assisted.[26] Former Secretary of Defense Donald Rumsfeld's comments serve to substantiate such concerns when he admitted that "it is quite true that 37,500 rations a day do not feed millions of human beings."[27] Unfortunately, the American mass media failed to follow up on these potential deaths, meaning that there is no way to know how many may have starved. Far from providing adequate assistance to the Afghan people, the U.S. food drops most likely did more harm than good since the American people were left with the false impression that the humanitarian crisis had been solved.

Much criticism of the war against Iraq coalesces around the alleged threat of Iraqi weapons of mass destruction. The largest of such criticisms maintained that the Bush administration never presented any concrete or irrefutable evidence of an Iraqi threat. Such an assertion has gained more weight in the United States, especially after David Kay, U.S. weapons inspector in Iraq, has announced that Iraq retains no known weapons of mass destruction.[28] Later comments by members of the Bush administration also revealed doubts concerning Iraq's supposed weapons. Former Secretary of State Colin Powell admitted that "what the regime was intending to do in terms of its use of the weapons, we thought we understood, we were simply wrong,"[29] while Rumsfeld explained that "it is possible Iraqi leaders decided they would destroy [weapons of mass destruction] prior to the conflict."[30]

Scott Ritter, former UN weapons inspector from 1991 to 1998, has been one of the most critical of the Bush administration. Ritter argues,

> The intelligence cited by the president has turned out to be either egregiously erroneous or simply pulled from thin air. The details so precisely set forth have turned out to be void of any substance. Did the president lie, or was the intelligence fundamentally flawed? Either case is disturbing. Either case is damning.[31]

Of course, time has proven Scott Ritter correct. Even former President Bush came to admit that fact. Some Iraqi exiles have also been quick to speak out against the war as well. Daoud Fakhri explains,

As the son of Iraqi exiles myself, please allow me to correct the erroneous impression that most Iraqi exiles are longing for Bush and Blair to do the "honourable" thing and attack Iraq. Most of us are in fact deeply worried about the coming war and are praying that by some miracle it does not happen. . . . Given that in the past both these countries [the United States and Great Britain] supported Saddam, glossed over his use of chemical weapons, and have presided over a sanctions policy that has led to the deaths of well over a half million Iraqi children, why should I now believe Bush and Blair when they say they have the best interests of the Iraqi people at heart?[32]

Putting aside the misleading claims that Saddam possessed weapons of mass destruction, it is also necessary to examine the validity of the "threat" of an Iraq that actually possessed such weapons and feasibly could attack the United States. Is this a valid justification for war? This logic suggests that the United States must attack any country that it *perceives* possesses weapons of mass destruction and *might* be a threat to the United States. If this were the case, the United States would have to invade any country that presented a threat to world peace, including North Korea, China, Russia, India, Pakistan, Israel, and, ironically, itself. In the past, this would have meant that the United States had to invade the Soviet Union as well.

American policy was historically dictated through "mutual assured destruction," meaning that the United States and the Soviet Union, both possessing massive amounts of nuclear warheads, could not attack each other without sparking a worldwide nuclear war. In 2003, the Bush administration acted as if this long-standing reality is not applicable to countries that possess weapons of mass destruction. However, mutual assured destruction is as large of a factor today as it was in the Cold War. Knowing full well that an attack on Iraq would lead to retaliation against American cities (even with just biological and chemical weapons), why would the Bush administration invade Iraq? The U.S. invasion of Iraq, then, can be explained only if one accepts the notion that the Bush administration knew that Iraq did not possess weapons of mass destruction.

Both the attacks of September 11 and the U.S. response are significant when considering the persistence of American global power. Many throughout the world, especially in the Middle East, have argued that the War on Terror is a cover-up for continued American unilateralism and empire building. Such critics of American foreign policy argue that the massive American bombings during this war, far from preventing terror, are actually a participation in human rights abuses.[33] Many cite the intentional bombing of Iraqi infrastructure, such as water purification facilities, as well as the bombing of residential areas as a display of American disregard to civilian casualties.[34] Even further, some claim that the main goals of the war against Iraq had nothing to do with weapons of mass destruction or democratizing Iraq but rather with controlling 10 percent of the world's oil reserves and fulfilling a regime change against a dictator who no longer played ball with American interests and demands. In sum, U.S. and Western media failed in their mission to inform the public. They failed to investigate and report. Instead, the media accepted the government's narrative. When it became clear that this narrative was inaccurate, the people in the United States demanded change by electing a new administration that promised change. But even with President Obama leading the United States, terrorism is likely to continue to grow and develop into a greater threat. That is because terrorism is often a reaction to some form of injustice.

ROOT CAUSES AND CONSEQUENCES OF TERRORISM

Terrorism did not come from nowhere or for no reason. Terrorism has deep root causes, as it does consequences. One cannot address its aftermath without looking at what causes it. This chapter has argued that terrorism is a result of the struggle for power. This has been seen historically in the rise of empires as well as with the violent reactions to those empires. The focus has been predominantly on state and imperial terror because both have, in effect, traditionally been the dominant form of terrorism. State and imperial terror can incite individual and group responses that are more than merely actions aimed at gaining national power. Terrorism can also be seen as a response of desperation, incited by injustice and oppression. The terrorist often feels deprived of some rights or maltreated or has some sense of altruism. In most cases, the terrorist believes that he or she is serving a greater cause that is just. Terrorism as a response of desperation can be generally labeled a short-term cause of violence. Individuals have certain basic wishes, needs, or instincts that, if frustrated, contribute to aggressive behavior that may give rise to violence and revolution. Lyford Edwards pointed to this explanation when he discussed the "four elemental types of wishes" and concluded that violence occurs when one or more of them are repressed.[35] Ted Robert Gurr examined how changing conditions stimulate people's behavior and their responses. As discussed in chapter 1, Gurr concluded that relative deprivation is a contributing factor to violence. In discussing terrorism as a weapon, Brian Crozier observed that "terrorism is a weapon of the weak," which he equated with the violence emanating from government actions. He wrote, "The violence of the strong may express itself in high explosives or napalm bombs. These weapons are no more discriminate than a hand-grenade tossed from a rooftop; indeed they will make more innocent victims."[36] Crozier would have been more accurate by arguing that terrorism is overwhelmingly a weapon of the strong (napalm, conventional bombing, and nuclear weapons), with nonstate terrorism as an act of desperation existing as a smaller part of worldwide terrorism.

An area usually neglected when examining the roots of terrorism concerns economic disparity and desperation. Generally, violence and terrorism thrive under conditions of injustice and inequality. Two of the foremost examples of terrorist conflicts that are driven largely by economic injustice include the Israeli subjugation of the Palestinian territories, which has devastated the economies of the Gaza Strip and the West Bank, and guerilla warfare operations conducted in opposition to the U.S. occupation of Iraq (an occupation conducted under the context of U.S.-supported sanctions that have destroyed Iraq's economy and led to hundreds of thousands of deaths). In the case of the Palestinian territories, relative deprivation plays a major role in promulgating the conflict between Israeli and Palestinian extremists. The post–World War II period saw the establishment of newly independent nation-states (formerly Western colonies). Necessary in this process was the migration of dreams concerning aspirations for national independence throughout the world. Under this reality, many Palestinians felt and continue to feel that they have been denied their right to establish their own national home—their own Palestinian state. In the case of Iraq, the migration of dreams—specifically in the form of the "spread of democracy"—has encouraged many Iraqis to resist U.S. occupation in an effort to establish a fully independent Iraqi state free of American influence or control. Efforts at full independence have met stiff resistance by the U.S. government, in turn contributing to increased conflict between American "liberators" and Iraqi nationalists.

Scholars have produced many volumes dissecting the reasons individuals and groups resort to violence. It may be useful to look at some of those individuals to find out what they have to say about why they resorted to violence and terrorism. At the height of Palestinian airplane hijackings in the late 1960s and early 1970s, the late Dr. George Habash of the Popular Front for the Liberation of Palestine (PFLP), then leader of one of the groups that carried out such acts, defended them in the following manner:

> When the Jews were doing this sort of thing [terrorism] in Palestine you did not call it acts of terrorism, but a war of liberation . . . the attacks of the Popular Front are based on quality, not quantity. We believe that to kill a Zionist far from the battleground has more of an effect than killing 100 of them in battle; it attracts more attention. And when we set fire to a store in London, those few flames are worth the burning down of two kibbutzim. You have to be constantly reminded of our existence. After all, world opinion has never been either with us or against us; it has just kept ignoring us. . . . Where was the world opinion in 1917 when the British decided to give land that was ninety percent populated by Palestinians as a gift to the Jews?[37]

A member of the Popular Front for the Liberation of Palestine (PFLP), Leila Khaled was one of the earliest Palestinian hijackers. She defended her hijacking of the El Al Israeli passenger plane by arguing that her act should not be evaluated in isolation of the situation, underlying causes behind it, or on the basis of the Western value system, "which forgives the enemy of all crimes and considers me an outlaw."[38] Similarly, the Provisional Irish Republican Army (PIRA) argued for many years that terrorism and "the melodrama of the hunger strikes offer the only ways available with which to destabilize British imperial control of the province."[39] The PIRA hoped that such acts would make it too expensive for the British to keep controlling Northern Ireland. Palestinian Hamas activists often point to the violence of the enemy as the root cause of their terrorism. One such activist told the Israeli daily

Ha'aretz, "Israelis don't respect the lives of our civilians; they kill civilians, so why should we respect the lives of their civilians?"[40]

These passages substantiate an already well-known fact: the violence of terror often brings about more deadly violence against those who plan it, support it, or are affiliated with it. While terrorism itself is a reaction to perceived forms of violence and oppression, the act of terror seems to always bring about a violent reaction by the governments whose interests were attacked. Consequently, a cycle of violence starts with the act of terrorism. As the government responds with deadly violence, the terrorists respond to the government's response, and the cycle sets in. This pattern has been established in conflicts throughout the world, including those between Chechnya and Russia, Israel and the occupied territories, and the Colombian guerillas and the paramilitaries and possibly in the future relationship between al Qaeda and the United States (examples that will be discussed in chapter 4).

Another consequence of terrorism is the rise of a new phenomenon in wealthier societies. Even though short-lived, terrorism has the immediate impact of social cohesion. People affected by the violence of terror spontaneously join together to help out the victims and their relatives. In a way, everyone becomes a victim and feels an affinity with all other victims. Stories of people joining to help out in the aftermath of September 11 are abundant. In the same society where a neighbor barely knew other neighbors, everyone becomes a relative and a neighbor. In the aftermath of September 11, Americans joined together in raising the flag. The rush on flags was so great that many stores ran out. Under the slogan of "United We Stand," people everywhere joined in harmonious patriotism that unified the nation in ways not seen before.

Thus, along with social cohesion comes an enhanced sense of patriotism. Both oppressed and attacked societies experience this phenomenon. It is a known fact that when people are under attack, they tend to rally around the flag. The cycle of violence that follows a terrorist attack tends to enhance patriotism in those areas that receive the brunt of that violence. In the United States, there were more flags displayed in the aftermath of the September 11 attacks than had been seen in decades. This enhanced sense of patriotism, however, does not last long. In time, fear dissipates and routine sets back in. When the state from which the attack may have originated is threatened with attack itself, it also experiences a similar but temporary phenomenon.

The rise of patriotism, in turn, often contributes to the success of right-wing or conservative parties in later elections. In Israel, for example, the Likud coalition emerged on top almost every time in the aftermath of sustained Palestinian attacks. In the United States, the Republican Party made major and historic gains in the congressional elections of 2002 following the atmosphere of heightened security concerns after September 11 attacks and in the 2004 presidential election. In India as well as in Pakistan, similar consequences of terrorism were evident.

The economic consequences of terrorism and the cycles of violence that result are staggering. The costs of a terrorist attack go beyond the loss of life, however tragic that is. Such attacks usually have serious economic consequences for any society. Consumer spending, travel and tourism, the cost of insurance, new construction safeguards, and the cost of security all play a role in the economic consequences of terrorism. The cost of retaliation or a War on Terror is hard to measure but could have significant short-term economic consequences, especially considering the enormous cost of stationing the American military for a long-term military occupation of Iraq.

Civil rights also suffer when attempting to enhance domestic security. In the country that is attacked by terrorism, civil rights are often sacrificed when attempting to prevent further attacks. Both the passing and implementation of the USA Patriot Act, which potentially violates constitutional protections under the Bill of Rights,[41] and the unlawful detainment of over 1,000 Muslim Americans after September 11[42] display the increasing erosion of civil liberties in the War on Terror. The states from which terrorism originates also heighten their security in anticipation of retaliatory action, and the few civil rights they may have disappear. In Israel, Palestinian attacks have contributed to major setbacks in civil rights of citizens and noncitizens alike. Concurrently, Palestinian terrorist attacks have provided Israel the justification to demolish the houses of those who are related to suspected terrorists. In Britain, Northern Irish attacks contributed to similar trends toward limiting civil liberties.

Terrorism, no matter how abhorrent, also contributes to mutual awareness between the two parties involved. Citizens of the attacked country often become more aware of the other's concerns. After the September 11 attacks, Americans began to learn more about Islam, the Middle East, and the poverty of Afghanistan. Afghans, Muslims, and Arabs also humanized the other. They saw civilian casualties and learned about the lives they left behind. The outrage over the human tragedy was almost universal.

Mutual awareness often contributes to internal opposition. Citizens in the attacked society may begin to question the wisdom of their own government's response or policies. Those in the society where the attack originated may start to question the wisdom of such attacks. In the United States, opposition to attacking Afghanistan started almost immediately after such plans became public. Plans to attack Iraq received even wider opposition. Similarly, Israel has a vibrant opposition to its counterattacks in the Palestinian occupied territories. Importantly, the majority of Israelis and Palestinians support a two-state solution rather than a continuation of Israeli and Palestinian terrorist attacks.[43]

The continued cycle of violence often leads to third-party intervention and efforts to find a mutually acceptable way to end the violence. Such interventions have occurred after every major outbreak of violence in the Middle East, in Northern Ireland, and in Kashmir. If the government under attack is unable to control the violence and end its sources rapidly, the deteriorating situation invites third parties to help in finding face-saving formulas that both sides could live with.

CONCLUSION

Both globalization and terrorism are not new. They did not start with the fall of the Soviet Union or with the horrors of September 11. Both have deep roots in history. Both globalization and terrorism have multiple meanings, causes, and consequences. The recent trends in economic and political globalization have contributed to greater opportunities as well as deprivation. Today, our world thrives more on pursuing power rather than justice. In the process, globalization may have covered up many injustices and proliferated the migration of dreams. This process has enhanced the prospects for violent reactions by those who feel deprived of justice or even an alternative forum of expression. Such violent reactions have surely entailed terrorism. State-sponsored terror has also incited terrorist responses by those in opposition to foreign occupation and to their own governments' human rights abuses.

The violence of all forms of terrorism often contributes to the migration of nightmares and to greater violence emanating from those who are terrorized. A cycle of violence usually takes both sides into a phase of enhanced patriotism where emotion rather than reason dominates and right-wing leaders emerge or increase their power. Economic hardships and suppression of normal civil liberties follow. In time, however, hope sets in as opposition grows and third parties intervene.

CHAPTER 3

PALESTINE

We know that the official attitude toward terrorism suffers from a suspension of any inquiry into causation. Government officials seldom ask what causes terror or question their own participation in terrorist acts. Somehow one gets the feeling that there is no connection between terrorism and its root causes. This chapter challenges that sentiment and provides an example of causation. Perpetrators of terror are not simply born with some terrorist disease. Instead, specific conditions drive them to it. It is appropriate now to take a look at a prominent case where violence is a reaction to such circumstances.

PALESTINIAN VIOLENCE:
CAUSES AND CONSEQUENCES

While Palestinian resistance is generally seen as a reaction to the creation of the state of Israel in 1948, its causes have deep roots at many levels. First, it is a response to Zionist colonization of Palestine. Second, it is driven by psychological motivation to recover lost rights. Third, and perhaps most important, Palestinian resistance took root in the absence of meaningful peaceful channels for legitimate change. If Palestinians were given peaceful means for achieving justice, they were and are not likely to feel the need for revolutionary resistance.

It is, therefore, the unique circumstances that the Palestinian Arabs have faced that molded them into the culture of resistance through a variety of methods. The highlight of their resistance was the 1987–1993 intifada (uprising) and the second intifada that started in 2000. But the intifada was not a transitory phenomenon that sprang up from nowhere. Rather, it represented the acceleration of an ongoing process of resistance. Thus, it reflected continuity as it did innovation in the long struggle of the Palestinian Arabs in their quest for justice and independence.

PALESTINIAN RESISTANCE:
HISTORICAL BACKGROUND

The rise of Arab nationalism in Palestine paralleled its development among other Arabs. With the defeat of the Ottoman Empire at the hands of the Allied forces in 1918, Arab expectations of independence and unity were high. After the 1918 armistice, the Arabs came to be aware of the conflicting promises and felt a deep sense of betrayal.

The year 1917 marked a turning point in the history of Palestine as the globalization of the Palestinian-Jewish conflict incorporated an outside colonial power. This year witnessed the issuance of the Balfour Declaration and the beginning of British rule. In December 1917, General Allenby's forces entered Jerusalem and set up a British military administration in Palestine. On the basis of previous British promises, the Arabs of Palestine welcomed Allenby as a liberator, hoping that they would soon attain independence within a larger Arab state. These hopes were soon dashed, as the British began working on a program to place Palestine under their mandate. Moreover, the Balfour Declaration, promising British support for the creation of a "Jewish national home" in Palestine, was incorporated into the mandate resolution of the League of Nations in 1922.

Arab nationalism in Palestine was now rapidly taking shape in response to British rule and Zionist plans for their homeland. By the 1930s, their resistance manifested itself in organized political and armed activities. During this decade, Palestinian Arabs witnessed the emergence of their earliest guerilla groups. In addition, a number of political parties were formed. All these parties, regardless of loyalty or ideology, advocated national independence and opposed political Zionism, which aimed at creating a Jewish state in Palestine.

It was during the 1930s that the notion of popular armed struggle emerged in Palestine. One of the earliest such groups was the movement of Shaykh Izz el-Din al-Qassam. Qassam was able to mobilize a peasant following and train them in the use of arms. He advocated Arab unity and independence for Palestine. Qassam also vowed to wage armed struggle against the British and the Zionists. Qassam's very first act of violence included tossing a grenade on a Jewish home in the Nahalal colony in December 1932.[1] But before he could get his revolt going, the British ambushed Qassam and a dozen of his followers. Instead of surrendering or escaping, Qassam fought to the end. He and some of his followers were killed in battle on November 19, 1935.

Qassam's death made him a symbol of self-sacrifice and martyrdom, contributing to the spread of his ideals across the country. It was his followers who actually began the campaign of armed struggle and organized, with others, the famous Arab Revolt of 1936. That revolt represented the climax of Palestinian resistance during the mandate. It lasted until 1939 and was seen by the British as a major revolution to be suppressed. It is estimated that 5,000 Palestinians were brutally killed by British forces and Zionist militias during this period.[2] British behavior often bordered on terrorism. For example, in May 1936, the British authorities carried out heavy punitive measures, including demolishing a large section of the most significant Arab city, Jaffa. Residents lost their homes and properties in this massive form of collective punishment. In the same year, the British also began detaining suspects, mostly civilians, without trial.[3] While the revolt officially ended in 1939, violence persisted.

As Europe was self-destructing during World War II, Palestine was feeling the ramifications of European activities. New waves of immigrants, legal and illegal, were arriving in the country to escape Nazi terror. The Zionist enterprise, moreover, gained further international support and was solidified in the face of Hitler's plans for the Jews of Europe. In Palestine, Zionist violence grew to new heights and effectively divided the country into Jewish and Arab domains. In September 1944, for example, many attacks took place. On September 27 alone, four attacks on police stations took place, killing and injuring many innocent people. Two days later, an expert on Jewish affairs was murdered by a group called "Fighters for the Freedom of Israel." In October of the same year, many attacks were made on the Palestine railway system, and many railway employees were killed. On November 6 of the same year, Lord Moyne and his British driver were assassinated by the same group.[4]

The violence continued unabated after the end of World War II. In 1947, the British government announced, after many attempts at a solution, that "the mandate has proved to be unworkable in practice, and that the obligations undertaken to the two communities have shown to be irreconcilable."[5] By this time, the conflict between Arabs and Zionists had truly become irreconcilable. Palestine's Jewish population had reached 30 percent and had become a formidable force in the country.

It was at this juncture that the United Nations began to play an important part in the globalization of the Palestinian-Zionist conflict. The General Assembly delegated a special committee to travel to Palestine and investigate the situation. The report submitted by the UN Special Commission on Palestine (UNSCOP) incorporated two proposed plans: partition and federation. The majority of UNSCOP members favored the first plan to partition the country into two states: Jewish and Palestinian Arab. The minority of UNSCOP members favored a federal state in Palestine. To ensure the passage of the majority plan, Zionist pressures were applied inside and outside the United Nations. As U.S. President Truman confirmed, "So much lobbying and outside interference has been going on in this question [the partition plan] that it is almost impossible to get a fair-minded approach to the subject."[6] Later, Truman reminisced, "As the pressure mounted, I found it necessary to give instructions that I did not want to be approached by any more spokesmen for the extreme Zionist cause."[7]

The Arabs of Palestine did not have the means to counteract the Zionist lobbying activities in the United States or other countries. In the United States, politicians found it expedient to capitalize on Jewish concerns about the Nazi victims. The Arabs had no such appeal. Moreover, the Zionists had the necessary organizational infrastructures in the United States, while the Arabs had none. In addition, many Americans viewed the notion of a Jewish state in Palestine as a fulfillment of biblical prophecies. Thus, on November 29, 1947, the General Assembly adopted the partition plan.

According to this plan, Palestine was to be divided into six parts, three of which (56 percent of the total area) were to become a Jewish state and the other three (43 percent) an Arab state. Jerusalem and surrounding areas were to fall under UN administration. This resolution meant that the Jewish state would include 498,000 Jews and 497,000 Arabs (excluding the nomadic inhabitants of the Negev) and that the Arab state would include 725,000 Arabs and 10,000 Jews.

The Palestinian leadership rejected the partition resolution. They argued that it violated the provisions of the UN Charter on self-determination. The Palestinian rejection also was based on demographic and legal ownership facts. In the proposed Jewish state, half the population was to be Palestinian Arab, while its Jewish population owned less than 10 percent of its total land area.

THE CREATION OF ISRAEL

The reaction to the partition resolution among the Palestinians resulted in a wave of protests, demonstrations, and disturbances throughout Palestine. Soon after the adoption of the resolution, British forces began to withdraw from specific areas. Both Arabs and Zionists attempted to gain control of those areas, leading to attacks on local inhabitants. For example, on the night of December 18, 1947, vehicles loaded with armed Jewish men from the nearby settlements of Dan and Dasne attacked the Arab village of Khisas. The attackers threw grenades at the homes of the sleeping residents and withdrew, killing ten (including children) and wounding five.[8] As historian Edgar O'Ballance testified, "It was the Jewish policy to encourage the Arabs to quit their homes," and "they ejected those who clung to their villages."[9] Other Arabs, according to Sir John Bagot Glubb, were "encouraged to move by blows or by indecent acts."[10] Ethnic purification was so important to Zionist planners because of the demographic factors involved. Given that Jews were less than 30 percent of the population of all Palestine and a mere 50 percent in their allocated Jewish state—and given the high birthrate among the Arabs—it was imperative to rid their forthcoming state of as many Arabs as possible. Otherwise, the Jewish state would have an Arab majority in a very short time.

Confronted with the tragic situation in Palestine, the leading champion of partition, the United States, began to have second thoughts. Consequently, the United States submitted an alternative proposal to the UN Security Council on March 19, 1948. It proposed a temporary UN trusteeship over all of Palestine.

As the United Nations was reexamining the question of Palestine, Zionist planners were busy establishing their authority on the land of Palestine. As Dr. Chaim Weizmann, president of the World Zionist Organization, reminisced, "Our only chance now . . . was to create facts, to confront the world with these facts, and to build on their foundation." Later he was able to proclaim that "while the United Nations was debating trusteeship, the Jewish state was coming into being."[11] The most frequently mentioned incident among the many contributing to a panic flight of the Palestinian inhabitants was the terrorist massacre of Deir Yassin. On April 9, 1948, 254 men, women, and children in the village of Deir Yassin were massacred by Irgun attackers. The Irgun was a militant Zionist group led by Menachem Begin, who became Israel's prime minister in 1977. Under British rule in Palestine, Begin was a wanted terrorist. His group, the Irgun, committed hundreds of acts of violence targeting both civilian and public sites. The Irgun also involved itself in assassinations and sabotage. Such incidents contributed to a massive exodus of the Palestinian Arab population and opened the door for the creation of the Jewish state. Short of this Arab exodus, the Jewish state would have been demographically more Arab than Jewish.

The state of Israel was proclaimed in mid-May 1948. This newly born state incorporated not only the area specified to it in the partition resolution but also an enlarged area that it had just occupied. It was at this juncture that the Arabization of the Palestine conflict occurred. Prior to the establishment of Israel, volunteers and donations, besides diplomatic moves, characterized Arab involvement. But after the declaration of Israel and the mass exodus of Palestinians into neighboring

Arab countries, Arab armies entered Palestine. But the Arab offensive was weak and lacked coordination and leadership. The Israelis, on the other hand, were better prepared in terms of unity, organization, leadership, and sophistication. Even their numbers exceeded those of the Arab armies. They soon were on the offensive and were able to arrange for armistice agreements, as Israel had gained more territory (almost 80 percent of the land of former Palestine). Jordan took control of the remaining part of Palestine, including the old city of Jerusalem, with the exception of the Gaza district, which went to Egyptian control.

Thus, a Jewish state was established in Palestine. The Palestinian Arabs were left without a state and, for the majority of them, without homes. Their country was transformed into a state for others. The loss of the land of the forefathers and their refugee status left the Palestinians in a perpetual state of shock. In their memories, 1948 stands as the year of Nakba (catastrophe). Ever since, the notion of the return to the homeland has been a Palestinian obsession.

Therefore, Palestinian political culture began to center on rejection: the rejection of their disinheritance as well as the rejection of the status quo. It was in this context that Palestinian political culture became a culture of resistance and rebellion. Their resistance evolved through four distinct phases. Initially, the Palestinians resisted the existing Arab order. Their activists and intellectuals attempted to redirect the Arab system toward a more progressive and nationalist order. They argued that the catastrophe became possible because of Arab backwardness. The failure of the new Arab order, as exemplified in the 1967 Arab-Israeli war, led the Palestinians toward a more independent form of resistance. They began a campaign of armed and, in many cases, terrorist struggle on their own. As limitations of armed struggle became clear in the 1980s, Palestinians moved in the direction of mass rebellion. By the early 1990s, this rebellion was slowed substantially by the promise of a peace process. The failure of this process soon reignited a new wave of violence and terrorism.

THE FIRST PHASE: 1948–1967

In the period immediately following their diaspora, Palestinian intellectuals believed that the remedy for their plight rested on Arab unity. Some discussed modernization as a prerequisite to unity.[12] As one author put it, Arab leaders "showed naïveté in politics" and "weakness in diplomacy."[13]

To bring about modernization and unity, many Palestinians felt that the first step would be to change the traditional leadership, whom they felt had betrayed their cause. In July 1951, a Palestinian Arab assassinated King Abdullah of Jordan in Jerusalem. The assassination was in reaction to the general feeling among many Palestinians that the king had betrayed the Palestinian cause. In addition, most Palestinians hailed the overthrow of King Farouk of Egypt in 1952 and became the most enthusiastic supporters of Egypt's revolutionary leader, Gamal Abdul Nasser.

Nasser championed the cause of Arab unity. His ability to nationalize the Suez Canal and confront Britain, France, and Israel made him extremely popular among the Palestinians. His call for an Arab summit in 1964 led to the decision to establish a Palestinian organization. The early phase of the Palestine Liberation Organization under Ahmad Shukairy emphasized Arab joint efforts and the Arab character of Palestine.

In this phase, therefore, Palestinian political culture was shocked by what they called "the catastrophe" and looked for its causes. The other, rather than the self, was viewed as the culprit. The weak Arab order became the focus of Palestinian detestation. Remedies to this weak order rested with the Arabs. Salvation, therefore, awaited the reordering of Arab political affairs. The hope for return to their homes and lands from which they were dispossessed became a dream and an obsession. In time, the mystique of return became the single most important characteristic of Palestinian political culture. More than a bit ironic, then, was the fact that just as Zionism was achieving its zenith, a "Palestinian Zionism" was being born. Just as early Zionists looked for outside powers to help them bring about their version of the "Return," Palestinians at this early stage looked for help from the Arab governments. In time, especially after 1967, the Palestinians lost hope in being able to achieve their goals through the Arab states and felt that their only recourse was self-reliance through revolutionary violence and guerilla warfare. Thus, by the end of 1967, Palestinian political culture had entered its second phase.

THE SECOND PHASE: 1967–1987

The war of 1967 brought about a reawakening among the Palestinians. The Arabs, they learned, are unable to bring about their "Return." The speedy and devastating defeat of the combined forces of Egypt, Syria, and Jordan left most Palestinians in shock. In six days, Israel had quadrupled its size and come to occupy the remainder of Palestine (Jerusalem, the West Bank, and Gaza) as well as lands from neighboring Arab states (the Golan Heights and the Sinai peninsula). More than a third of the Palestinians were now faced with the enemy as their occupying master. During the earlier phase, Palestinian political culture was characterized by its emphasis on the lost homeland and the dream of "Return." It was alienation from the homeland that gave Palestinians their most powerful common cultural bond, reinforcing the belief that Israel was responsible for the brunt of Palestinian suffering.

After the defeat of 1967, Palestinians began to combine their longing for the "Return" with an emphasis on the maintenance of their identity. Thus, Palestinian nationalism began to replace the traditional Arab nationalism, which dominated Palestinian political culture prior to 1967. This emphasis on identity was necessitated by the war and its consequences. The 1967 war was an Arab-Israeli war in which the Palestinian dimension was almost totally absent. Israel, for the first time, came to occupy lands from neighboring Arab states. These states now had a new priority regarding Israel: the liberation of lost lands. The UN Security Council resolution addressing the war and the resolution of the conflict (Resolution 242) advocated an exchange of occupied land for peace. The resolution has been criticized because it makes no mention of the Palestinian people except as refugees and fails to make any reference to a Palestinian state. Israeli leaders were boldly denying the existence of a Palestinian people, as in the case of Golda Meir's infamous speech of 1969 in which she said, "It was not as though there was a Palestinian people in Palestine considering itself as a Palestinian people and we came and threw them out and took their country away from them"; the Israeli prime minister after 1967 proclaimed, "They did not exist."[14] In addition, Israeli occupation authorities were busily strangulating Palestinian expression in the West Bank and the Gaza Strip. Together, these activities prompted Palestinians everywhere to emphasize their own identity.

Emphasis on Palestinian national identity required alternative means for the liberation of the lost homeland. If dependence on the Arabs was no more an avenue, then a different one had to be found. For a decade earlier, small groups of Palestinians had already argued for guerilla warfare as the means for the weak Palestinians to struggle against the strong Israelis. Their calls, however, were mere whispers, and Palestinians everywhere continued to look to the Arabs for a solution. The shattering Arab defeat in 1967 radically affected perceptions of the Arabs and helped create the political atmosphere in which guerilla warfare became the preferred alternative means of liberation. Guerilla warfare and armed struggle had already been successfully practiced in Algeria and was being waged in Vietnam and other places with some success. With such vivid examples of weak peoples resisting seemingly invincible enemies, the Palestinian masses turned rapidly in that direction.

The popularity of armed struggle was further reinforced after the battle of Karameh in March 1968. On March 21, 1968, Israel launched a massive attack on the town of Karameh in Jordan. The objective of the Israeli incursion was to root out Palestinian commandos who made Karameh into a major center for training and launching attacks against it. Although the commandos, assisted by Jordanian forces, were outnumbered and suffered heavy casualties, they inflicted severe losses on the Israeli forces and were able to force the invaders to retreat. Pictures of burnt-out Israeli tanks and captured Israeli soldiers in newspapers and on television screens gave the commandos a major boost. Just months after Israel defeated the combined forces of Jordan, Syria, and Egypt, few armed commandos were able to inflict damage and "defeat" Israel in battle. Although hardly a military victory, the battle of Karameh was a major psychological victory for the notion of armed struggle. The ranks of the commandos swelled rapidly, and their popularity became ominous.

Soon after Karameh, Palestinian political culture became characterized by its admiration of the commandos, known in Arabic as fedayeen, or those who sacrifice themselves. Palestinian literature, art, songs, and media made the fedayeen into legendary heroes. Palestinian hopes were now fixed on the commandos as if, in a miraculous way, they will be able to transform these dreams into reality. The commandos' "victory" against Israel, like the Vietnamese and Algerian victories, contributed to the migration of dreams through the growth of guerilla movements across national borders. Consequently, the old pro-Arab leadership of the Palestine Liberation Organization (PLO) was replaced in favor of commando leaders; armed struggle replaced Arab military cooperation as the means of liberation in the PLO's charter. As mentioned earlier, small commando groups had been at work from before the 1967 war. The very first incursion was carried out on January 1, 1965, when a Palestinian commando crossed into Israel and placed explosives that destroyed a section of the pipeline designed to divert the waters of the Jordan River into Israel. After the 1967 War, infiltrations intensified and often aimed at economic targets, including tourist buses. But Palestinian armed struggle had its limitations. The Palestinian commandos were based in sovereign Arab states, and it soon became obvious that Palestinian interests were not always compatible with the interests of their host states. In time, Palestinian commandos took their battle into the global arena. They began to hijack Israeli and Western airplanes and make demands on Israel. Heavy Israeli retaliation in Arab lands where the commandos originated led to more Arab military pressure against the commandos. In time, occasional clashes with Arab security forces gave way to full-fledged civil wars that Palestinian commandos were destined to lose.

With every clash and every civil war, Palestinian nationalism was strengthened even though the commandos usually lost. By the early 1980s, Palestinian commandos, had been driven out of Jordan, faced fierce attacks by Lebanese army and militia units, and confronted occasional Syrian onslaughts. Yet their guerilla incursions into Israel continued. It was these incursions that brought on the commandos the wrath of the Israelis. In June 1982, Israel invaded Lebanon in order to drive the commandos out of the country. Palestinian steadfastness, patience, and heroism were unable to reverse the inevitable. Israel's occupation of south Lebanon, its siege of Beirut, and its devastating and constant shelling of Lebanon's capital, including deliberate or indiscriminate or reckless bombardment of a civilian character, of hospitals, schools and other non-military targets,[15] for about three months forced the Palestinians to accept an internationally brokered agreement. Accordingly, the commandos were dispersed into other Arab states, and the PLO headquarters were moved to Tunis. These developments led some Palestinians to question the viability of armed struggle as the major agent of liberation. This new mode became dominant by the end of 1987 with the start of the third phase: the intifada.

THE THIRD PHASE: 1987–1993

The Palestinian intifada (uprising) was motivated by Israeli behavior as well as by commando failures. The dimmed hopes of liberation by fedayeen coming from neighboring countries did entice many Palestinians to search for alternative means. This affected especially Palestinians living under Israel's occupation and having to endure its hardships and witness its progress.

While Israel's victory over its Arab neighbors in 1967 provided it an opportunity to achieve a lasting peace in the area, Israel instead chose to establish its expansion of its sovereignty to include the West Bank and the Gaza Strip. Contrary to the principles of international law, Israel set out to Judaize the areas. Doing so required the suppression of the very identity of the Palestinian people. Therefore, it was natural for Israel's leaders to deny the very existence of the Palestinian people. Golda Meir's infamous statement after the 1967 war that "they did not exist" was followed by Menachem Begin's warning at a kibbutz in 1969:

> My friend, take care. When you recognize the concept of "Palestine," you demolish your right to live in Ein Hahoresh. If this is Palestine and not the land of Israel, then you are conquerors and not tillers of the land. You're invaders. If this is Palestine, then it belongs to a people who lived here before you came.[16]

The 1967 victory, therefore, was not a victory over another people but a war to "liberate" Israel's lands. Israeli government publications asserted that "in the course of the Six-Day War new territories to the north, center, and south of the former boundaries of the State of Israel were liberated."[17] This attitude was strengthened with the assumption of the Likud Party to power in 1977. Menachem Begin, as Israel's prime minister, was even more vehement in his rejection of reality when he said, "The term West Bank means nothing. It is Judea-Samaria. It is Israeli land belonging to Jewish people."[18]

Israeli leaders would like the world to believe the land belongs to Israel so that its inhabitants can be denied their national identity or the right thereof to express such identity. When one surveys the political motivation and Israel's strangulation of Palestinian political expression, one concludes that Israeli policies and practices do perpetuate the denial of self-determination to the Palestinian people and an expansionist design aimed at securing a monopoly over the whole of geographic Palestine.

Israel's designed strangulation of Palestinian political expression reaches the entire sphere of political and cultural life. At the political level, all modes of conventional political participation were blocked. Political parties were banned, elections were halted, and all forms of political activity were made illegal and punished severely. Cultural strangulation, on the other hand, was manifested in restrictions on freedom of expression, repression of education, suppression of literature and art, and the curtailment of symbolic national expression.

From the onset in 1967, Israel applied the Defense (Emergency) Regulations of 1945 in order to have the legal empowerment to carry out its policy of securing sovereignty over the occupied territories and suppressing Palestinian national aspirations. The application of these regulations constitutes a clear violation of international law prohibiting the occupier from making even temporary changes in the law of government of the occupied area.

The British Mandate government in 1945 introduced these regulations. Jacov Shimshon Shapira, who later became Israel's attorney general and minister of justice, attacked these same regulations, which he came to apply, as "uncivilized." In 1946, Shapira said,

> The system established in Palestine since the issue of the Defence Laws is unparalleled in any civilized country; there were no such laws even in Nazi Germany. It is our duty to tell the whole world that the Defense Law passed by the British mandatory government of Palestine destroys the very foundation of justice in this land.[19]

Justice, however, became less relevant to the Israeli minister of justice when the subjects were Palestinian Arabs. Consequently, Israeli suppression of Palestinian national, civil, and human rights goes unquestioned by Israeli officials. In fact, there are very few provisions in the various international covenants on human and civil rights that Israel has not violated repeatedly in its treatment of the population of the occupied territories. The life of every Palestinian living under Israel's occupation has therefore been touched and made more difficult.

Such practices as carrying identity cards, displaying different-color license plates, harassment at checkpoints, limitations on domestic and international travel, constructing a separation wall, and a host of other measures limiting personal and civil freedom have contributed to Israel's attempts at strangulating Palestinian nationalist expression.

Despite all such attempts at obstructing Palestinian political expression under occupation, the Palestinians of the occupied territories have given birth to alternative methods of expression. Today, their message is clear. They want the fulfillment of their national aspirations to self-determination and the establishment of an independent Palestinian state with Jerusalem as its capital. Their message, in practice, is a message of resistance to Israeli plans and of steadfastness on their land. This message has come across loud and clear since December 9, 1987, when the Palestinians in the occupied territories began their longest and most sustained intifada since Israel's occupation began in 1967. This uprising represented an acceleration of an ongoing process of resistance. As such, it did not represent an interruption of an order as much as it did the culmination of an order. It represented a natural development. In reality, the uprising was the natural response to an unnatural occupation, an occupation that has been condemned repeatedly as a flagrant violation of international law. Far away from the events, people reacted with surprise or shock, but there is nothing surprising or shocking about the refusal of a new generation of Palestinians to inherit pain and powerlessness or an old generation to accept the denial of their very existence as people.

Within days from the start of the December 9, 1987, intifada, the pro-PLO nationalist forces formed a joint command known as the United National Command for the Uprising (UNCU) and joined in Gaza by the new Islamic Jihad. Their leaflets, distributed clandestinely every other week or so, directed the masses and the support groups and put forth their message and demands. The leaflets, which have often been employed by the political forces, became the most powerful form of written political expression of the Palestinians under occupation. To those Palestinians, the leaflet was transformed into a sort of a biweekly constitution.

Signed by the UNCU/PLO, it told people when to go to work and when to strike, when to demonstrate, when to break curfews, when to go to schools, when to visit families of those killed or imprisoned, and a host of other activities. The leaflets also directed the support groups and the masses to organize neighborhood committees for education, welfare, health, and agriculture and to guard their neighborhoods. The mass support the leadership received made the Palestinian intifada a remarkable phenomenon in the history of the Palestinians and foiled Israel's attempts at crushing it.

The leaflets continuously asserted Palestinian demands to end the occupation and their right to self-determination. The link between the

Palestinians under occupation and the PLO was emphasized in every leaflet and by the fact that the leaflets themselves were signed by the UNCU of the PLO. The so-called Jordanian option, whereby Israel negotiates the future of the territories with Jordan, was also condemned in the leaflets. The Palestinians clearly wanted nothing less than their independence. The Jordanian king subsequently declared the death of the Jordanian option when he severed Jordan's administrative ties with the West Bank. By that time, however, the new administration had been in place. Popular committees were already running the new and clandestine apparatus of the Palestinians under occupation. As reported by John Kifner of the *New York Times* on May 15, 1988, "The Palestinians [had cut] themselves off from Israeli institutions and regulations."[20]

By then, the Palestinians in the occupied territories were, at the instructions of the UNCU, building self-sufficiency. Popular committees ran towns, villages, and refugee camps. Schools sprung up in homes, churches, and mosques. Yards and vacant lots were being cultivated. Potential blood donors were classified by blood type to prepare for emergencies. Makeshift clinics were created in camps, neighborhoods, and villages. Water wells were tested and treated as emergency water resources in case Israel cuts off water supplies. Landlords were forgiving rent payments. Security patrols with whistles and flashlights were set up to watch for attacks by settlers and the army. Food supplies were also stored in almost every neighborhood. In sum, the intifada was a clear manifestation of a social revolution that involved the entire Palestinian body politic.[21]

The Israelis were caught by surprise. Their leaders predicted the end of the intifada in a matter of days. Defense Minister Yitzhak Rabin even refused to interrupt a visit to the United States at the start of the intifada while assuring reporters that the uprising would die out in a matter of days. But the intifada intensified, as did Israel's repression. Consequently, Israel became polarized between those who argued for expulsion of the Palestinians and those who advocated the end of the occupation. But almost all Israelis, as evidenced by the statements of their leaders and the media, came to the conclusion that a return to the pre-intifada status quo was impossible. Thus, as a form of political expression, the intifada sent the Palestinian message to Israel, as it did the world.

The intifada had the immediate effect of redrawing the border between Israel and the occupied territories. With Israel's inability to put an early end to it, the intifada gave the Palestinians a new sense of empowerment. Especially in the aftermath of its forced departure from Lebanon, the Palestinian leadership could now engage the Israelis in negotiations from a position of perceived power rather than defeat. The intifada also forced the Israelis to rethink their position on the occupation itself. During the early years of the intifada, Israel found itself occupying the West Bank and Gaza but unable to rule there. Soldiers had to be dispatched in large numbers and became entangled with an unarmed civilian population that had lost the element of fear. Pictures of Israeli armed soldiers shooting at Palestinian teenagers were not comforting to many Israelis. Economically, the occupied areas also turned into a liability. Emotionally, Israel found itself drained. In a short time, the occupation became a major issue polarizing Israel's society as well as its body politic.[22] Consequently, Israel became more serious about finding alternatives to it occupation of the areas. Attention shifted toward establishing a Palestinian authority to administer the areas, while the land would remain effectively under Israeli control.

Important to both the Israeli and Palestinian leaderships was the rise of the Islamic movement under the banners of Hamas and Islamic Jihad.[23] While both of these groups existed in some form prior to the intifada, the uprising gave them new life and many recruits. The leadership of the PLO in Tunis feared their newfound popularity and saw them as competitors for Palestinian leadership. The Israeli leaders, on the other hand, initially attempted to use these groups to further divide the Palestinians under its occupation. Within a year, however, Israeli leaders became alarmed at the pace of growth of Hamas and Islamic Jihad as they went about their daring attacks on Israelis. Their attacks often included suicide bombings in which a belt of explosives is wrapped around a volunteer who infiltrates Israel and finds a crowded area to set the explosives off. Many of the volunteers are determined individuals who have some grievance. Take, for example, the case of Hanadi Jaradat, who carried out a suicide bombing at Maxim's restaurant in Israel, killing herself and twenty-one innocent victims. Hanadi was a well-educated twenty-nine-year-old attorney from the West Bank town of Jenin. Two weeks prior to her deadly attack, Israeli forces came to her family home looking for her brother. When located, her brother was shot and killed. Also killed in the attack was her fiancé. Both were killed while Hanadi watched. It was at that point that Hanadi approached Islamic Jihad activists to volunteer for the suicide bombing. Her subsequent action may have been motivated as much by revenge as by frustration. But her act led to the migration of Palestinian nightmares into Israeli society.

In time, Israeli leaders came to the realization that such groups pose a greater danger to their security than does the PLO. In fact, the activities of such Islamic revivalist groups made the PLO leadership look moderate to many Israelis. As such, both the Israeli and the Palestinian leaderships found in Hamas and Islamic Jihad a new common enemy that needed to be controlled. Thus, both Israel and the PLO sought alternatives to the status quo.

The Iraqi invasion of Kuwait in August 1990 and the subsequent war against Iraq gave the PLO yet another incentive to join an American-sponsored peace process. That war and its consequences contributed to the movement toward the peace process in many ways. First, the PLO found itself isolated from its financial benefactors in the Persian/Arabian Gulf and weakened diplomatically in its global relations. While the position of the PLO actually did not support the Iraqi occupation of Kuwait, its opposition to the international campaign to end that occupation was perceived in many circles as supportive of Iraq.[24] With the loss of Gulf funds, diplomatic setbacks, and more than 300,000 Kuwait Palestinians becoming dispossessed, the PLO became less able to help sustain the intifada and began to look for alternatives. The peace process was such an alternative.

The Gulf War of 1991 had serious impact on Israel as well. The war, in which Israel did not openly participate, destroyed the Israeli sense of security through defensible borders. For the first time in the history of Arab-Israeli wars, Arab missiles rocked the heart of Tel Aviv, shattering the myth that the West Bank provided Israel with a deep defensible border. That long-held Israeli argument for buffer zones came into question as Iraqi Scud missiles crossed over Jordanian and West Bank territories to hit targets deep inside Israel. Moreover, the fear that Iraqi missiles could have carried chemical and biological agents and the psychological impact of the distribution of gas masks to every Israeli made many Israelis aware that security is better provided through peace negotiations than the occupation of buffer zones.

A third ramification of that war had to do with the United States. The U.S. effort to dislodge Iraq from Kuwait was carried out under the banner of respect for international law and enforcement of UN Security

Council resolutions. Such a position, though, had the effect of exposing a U.S. double standard. The Israeli occupation of Arab lands violated the same set of international laws and elicited, over the years, many UN Security Council resolutions. The American policy had consistently protected Israel from international sanctions and provided it with military and economic support in order "to ensure Israeli military superiority over any combination of Arab states."[25] In order to maintain an Arab alliance against Iraq, the United States consequently promised to tackle the issue of Israeli occupation soon after the liberation of Kuwait. Coupled with the demise of the Soviet Union soon after the war, the U.S. commitment to settling the Arab-Israeli conflict became vital.

THE FOURTH PHASE:
THE "PEACE PROCESS" AND TERRORISM

Recent years have seen a focus on what is referred to as the peace process between Israel and the Palestinians of the occupied territories. While initiatives such as the Oslo Accords and the Camp David Accords and most recently the Bush administration's Road Map for Peace have all been treated as fair deals for both Israelis and Palestinians, the reality surrounding the peace process is radically different. Neither Oslo nor Camp David included any specific timetable for the creation of a sovereign Palestinian state. The Road Map for Peace requires Palestinians to "undertake an immediate cessation of violence"[26] before the creation of a sovereign Palestinian state will be considered, something no Palestinian leader can promise or enforce (all acts of terrorism cannot be prevented even under an authoritarian state). Neither Oslo, nor Camp David, nor the Road Map proposed a total end to the illegal Israeli settlements in the West Bank either, as some discussed a halt to further construction only. It is interesting, then, that the peace process contains none of the necessary components to actually promote a lasting peace between Israelis and Palestinians.

The Road Map for Peace is the most important of peace initiatives today, as it has been heralded as the new solution to the Israeli-Palestinian conflict. The Road Map, along with the most recent plans of Israeli leaders, provides no requisites for a truly sovereign or meaningful state. As mentioned, the majority of Israeli settlements in the West

Bank will not be dismantled. These settlements and the highways connecting them run throughout the entirety of the West Bank. The settlements threaten to divide the entire country into separate districts, with no way to travel from one to another without going through Israeli checkpoints. Furthermore, Ariel Sharon's plan for a Palestinian state will not include a Palestinian army or Palestinian control over its border and airspace. Israel will also continue with the building of the wall deep into the West Bank, threatening to further segregate the Palestinian people into a concentration camp style of confinement. It becomes increasingly obvious by looking at these characteristics for the Palestinian state that the Palestinians are being offered less than any rational human should accept. The creation of such a Palestinian state would be nothing more than a joke—a state by name but an occupied territory under Israeli jurisdiction and assault. Far from a plan for peace, the Road Map is a recipe for the indefinite subordination of the West Bank and the Gaza Strip and the maintenance of permanent Israeli territorial jurisdiction over those territories. The peace process has been criticized so strongly because it does not adequately deal with many of the Palestinian demands at the heart of the Israeli-Palestinian conflict: a mandatory and permanent withdrawal of Israeli control over Gaza and the West Bank, a guarantee for the creation of a sovereign Palestinian state in the near future, and the dismantlement of all the illegal Israeli settlements in the occupied territories. Without the fulfillment of these demands, it is unlikely that Palestinian or Israeli terrorist attacks will end in the foreseeable future.

The Israeli plan for permanent control of the West Bank should not be considered that controversial considering the incriminating statements of Israeli leaders themselves. Prime Minister Benjamin Netanyahu argued in his book *A Place among the Nations* for the permanent subjugation of the Gaza Strip and West Bank under Israeli dominance.[27] Former Prime Minister Menachem Begin, as already highlighted, claimed that the West Bank did not exist, while the Peres-Shamir coalition government added that no "additional Palestinian state" would be allowed to exist in the region,[28] Jordan supposedly being the first Palestinian state. Former Prime Minister Rabin said of the Palestinians, "The inhabitants of the Occupied Territories are subject to harsh military and economic pressure," alluding to his final promise that "in the end, they (Palestinians) will be broken."[29] Israel's current prime minister, Netanyahu, has a long history of support for settlement activities as well.

TERRORISM IN THE ISRAELI-PALESTINIAN CONFLICT

The Israeli-Palestinian conflict has been characterized by terrorist atrocities committed by both sides. These terror attacks demonstrate the full viciousness that accompanies the migration of nightmares between nations.

Palestinian terrorism, often taking the form of suicide bombings, has caused considerable destruction. Suicide bombings have incited fear and uncertainty in the minds of Israelis throughout the occupied territories and in Israel itself. Suicide bombings create so much fear because of their random nature; in effect, all Israelis are terrorized by the fear that they could lose their lives at any time. The stories of Moti Mizrachi and Daniel Turjeman indicate the dangers that Israelis face every day from suicide bombings. Mizrachi and Turjeman were attacked in a Jerusalem café in March 2002, injured by a suicide bombing. Mizrachi's and Turjeman's stories reveal the brutality of such attacks. Mizrachi explains, "There was an explosion. I fell to the floor. After a few seconds, I woke up. Everything around was torn apart. There was blood, body parts, people—water squirting from the ceiling, maybe from a burst pipe. I picked myself up to get help. I was bleeding heavily." Shrapnel barely missed Mizrachi's aorta, but his left hand was nearly severed. Mizrachi also suffered shrapnel wounds to his head. Mizrachi's hand, although now reattached, is held together by pins; he suffers tremendous pain and must make frequent visits to the hospital. Mizrachi's reaction is instructive in explaining the fear that Israelis bear: "One quick minute and everything is radically changed. It's like your life was erased—everything that you did vanished into nothing. I used to be active, to play soccer two or three times a week, I was on teams, I danced." Turjeman describes his experiences that day:

> Everything exploded. I flew twenty meters from the blast, literally across the road, and fell onto the street. I lost consciousness and came to after a few minutes. There was screaming and ambulances. I felt that my arm was not connected to my body. It was barely connected to my shoulder. The friend who had invited me that evening came looking for me. He

saw immediately that my arm was a mess. I also held one eye closed because it was full of metal. He asked me what was in his eye. I didn't want to tell him that his eye was hanging out, attached by just a few ligaments. It makes me sick to remember this.

All together, eleven Israelis were killed in this attack, and over fifty were seriously injured. Sadly, this bombing was only one of forty-eight suicide bombings against Israeli civilians between January 1, 2001, and August 31, 2002.[30]

The suicide bombings committed against Israeli civilians have been rightly condemned in the American mass media. Unfortunately, acts of Palestinian terror have been focused on to the exclusion of Israeli terrorist attacks. Israeli state terror, committed against the Palestinians as well as in retaliation for Palestinian attacks, has been tremendous. During the second intifada, Israeli murder has been considerable in cities such as Beit Jala, a Christian Palestinian town just south of Jerusalem. The area came under heavy rocket and artillery fire by the Israeli Defense Forces in response to purported Palestinian small-arms fire. Raphaella Fischer's story shows the despair that has been wrought on Palestinian cities by the Israeli military. Fischer describes the day her father was killed by the reckless Israeli shelling of their town:

> Looking back at the day when my father was taken away, I remember feeling that my soul was leaving to another zone. For some reason I couldn't understand, I felt like the whole world was going to end, so I screamed and felt I was going to die. In reality, a part of me is now missing and I'm cracked up with my misery.[31]

Israeli crimes committed during the second intifada were far from isolated incidents. Eyewitness accounts of the 2002 Israeli invasion of the West Bank implicate the Israeli army in the summary executions of Palestinian citizens. Sanna al-Sadi, widower to one of those executed in Jenin, recalls the incident:

> My husband [Abdelkarim Yusuf al-Sadi] and I had a very happy life together, although it was cut too short. During the invasion, I was at my in-laws' house with my husband. We were all sitting together as the area was being shelled by the Israelis. We constantly tried to comfort each other. During the first day, I spent time trying to cheer everyone up. Our

neighbors escaped to our house when the shells destroyed their home. Israeli soldiers came and blasted open the back gate. The Israelis stormed in. Abdelkarim my husband, Waddah al-Shalabi our neighbor, and his father were ordered to stand outside near a wall. They were ordered to lift up their arms while facing the wall. As they did so, the soldiers opened fire to execute all three of them. We knew that these three men had nothing to do with the resistance. We did not expect that they would be executed. I started screaming at the top of my lungs, "They have died, they have been martyred!" My husband was so innocent. He never hurt anyone. I was so terrified and humiliated. I immediately felt like I wanted to avenge my husband.[32]

Israeli terrorism has taken a substantial toll on the people of Gaza and the West Bank. All told, as many as 390 Palestinian men, women, and children died from Israeli repression during the initial year of the first intifada (1987) and more than 2,000 during the al Aqsa (second) intifada, a significant portion of both being civilian casualties.[33] The stories of the victims of Israeli-Palestinian terror reinforce the brutality of the migration of nightmares over national boundaries. Terrorist attacks like those committed by Palestinian suicide bombers and by the Israeli military reveal the suffering and emotions on both sides of the conflict that fuel the cycle of violence. These stories also substantiate the notion that such terrorist attacks are an ineffective way of increasing Israeli and Palestinian security.

MOTIVATIONS FOR ISRAELI AND PALESTINIAN TERRORISM

While terrorists do commit crimes against humanity, the official reaction is usually for retaliation, condemnation, investigation, and denunciation; there is usually little inquiry by government officials into why individuals or groups carry out such acts. It is hard to imagine a solution to a problem without addressing its root causes. Doing so would be like a doctor sewing a wound with an infection still flaring on the inside. It is this issue that we must turn to now.

The arguments in this book indicate that Israeli terrorism in Gaza and the West Bank has been conducted under the motivation of permanently subjugating these occupied territories under Israeli jurisdiction and control. Little else would describe Israel's continued and stubborn occupation of Palestinian lands for more than four decades in clear defiance of international law and at great cost to Israeli and Palestinian security and human rights. The refusal to remove Israeli settlements, Israel's wall within the West Bank, the damning statements of Israeli leaders condemning Palestinian rights, and the withholding of any substantive Palestinian state and necessary state sovereignty from the Palestinian people all indicate that Israel is not interested in a peaceful solution to this terrorist conflict. The continued use of violence in the attempt to destroy the Palestinian resistance confirms Israel's commitment to destroying any chance of Palestinian independence from foreign influence.

Palestinian terrorism against Israeli civilians is very likely of a different nature. While suicide bombings and other terrorist attacks are, at times, the product of the power struggle between organizations such as Hamas and Islamic Jihad and the state of Israel, Palestinian terrorist attacks (suicide bombings) are often a result of desperation. As Sanna al-Sadi (above) explained in the previous extract regarding her husband's death, "I was so terrified and humiliated. I immediately felt like I wanted to avenge my husband."[34] Sanna's reaction is enlightening in that it helps explain the motivations behind prospective terrorists with nothing left to lose. How many other Palestinian men, women, and children have suffered the fate of Sanni? How many of them are willing to take out their anger and frustration on Israeli civilians and military targets? As the persistence of the Israeli-Palestinian conflict demonstrates, as long as Israeli leaders find it necessary to continue their occupation and human rights abuses, the victims of those abuses will be ready to retaliate. The story of Hanadi Jaradat, who lost her brother and her fiancé before she became a suicide bomber, is a reminder that the cycle of terror rarely begins with one individual terrorist.

GLOBALIZATION AND DOMINATION: PUTTING THE ISRAELI-PALESTINIAN CONFLICT INTO PROPER CONTEXT

An analysis of the Israeli-Palestinian conflict would not be complete without discussion of the U.S. role in supporting Israeli atrocities. The American mass media has done an excellent job of burying and censoring Israeli terrorism, thereby erasing American responsibility for Israel's actions. For those who look beyond the U.S. media, the picture that emerges is quite clear. The leading recipient of American foreign aid is Israel, receiving more than $3 billion a year. American aid to Israel goes, among other things, to the purchase of American military weapons, including tanks, helicopters, bombers, machine guns, and bullets. These weapons are used repeatedly in Israeli human rights abuses committed against Palestinians in the occupied territories. American aid also goes to protecting thousands of Israeli settlers living illegally in Jerusalem and the West Bank. It would be difficult if not impossible for the Obama administration (or past administrations) to argue that they are not aware of Israeli human rights abuses. This would mean that American leaders have continued their support of Israel despite its crimes.

Explanations for American support for Israel vary. However, if one is to accept the seriousness of Israeli terrorism committed in the occupied territories, then it is difficult to escape the conclusion that the Israeli assault serves some sort of geopolitical realist American interest. This would not be the first time that the United States has used client regimes with dismal human rights records to further its political interests. Proponents of this explanation maintain that American support for Israel, coupled with support for Saudi Arabia and now Iraq, reinforce American hegemony in the Middle East and control of strategic economic resources. Such critics cite American military presence throughout the world, unprecedented in world history until now, to substantiate the existence of American empire. If the realist explanation of American support for Israel is true, it may mean the indefinite migration of nightmares from the United States to the occupied territories in the form of Israeli repression. The consequences include a countermigration of nightmares from the Palestinian grim reality to Israel and its benefactor.

SIGNS OF HOPE: THE GLOBALIZATION OF NONVIOLENCE IN THE OCCUPIED TERRITORIES

The use of nonviolent tactics as seen in the first and second intifada is encouraging for those who support a nonviolent solution to the American-Israeli-Palestinian conflict. The migration of dreams through the globalization of nonviolent resistance to government repression is now evident, including Gandhi in India, the civil rights movement in the United States, the nonviolent resistance to South African apartheid, and now the resistance in the occupied territories. Palestinian successes with the use of nonviolence may lead to considerable gains for the Palestinian people. The use of nonviolence may be essential in changing world opinion (particularly in the United States) concerning the nature of the Israeli occupation. Success may also help in removing Israeli leaders' justification for use of force in the Gaza Strip and the West Bank. Nonviolent tactics may help bring about an end to the cycle of violence and remove the justification in the minds of Israelis and those throughout the world who believe that Israeli repression is a legitimate means of self-defense. Furthermore, success in any of these areas will be necessary in order to make any significant progress toward the establishment of a sovereign Palestinian state.

Just like with terrorism, both Israelis and Palestinians have carried out nonviolent action. Some Israelis have even refused military service in Gaza or the West Bank in objection to the occupation, preferring jail to service. Some Palestinians and international supporters have lost their lives demonstrating for an end to the occupation. Many forms of nonviolent resistance have been practiced in opposition to Israel's occupation and its behavior. On December 28, 2003, Israeli Gil Na'amati, from Kibbutz Re'em in the Negev, was protesting with other Israelis, foreigners, and Palestinians. They were making known their opposition to the construction of the so-called security fence. When Israeli soldiers arrived at the scene, they opened fire. A number of demonstrators were injured. Among them was Gil, who suffered serious injuries. Gil was not the first Israeli to suffer because of his opposition to the occupation, and he will not be the last. But it is acts of courage such as Gil's, along with international volunteers and Palestinian civilians, that give us a glimpse of hope for the future. Perhaps the nightmares of the day will be transformed into pleasant dreams of peace and reconciliation between Israelis and Palestinians. Hope, however, seems remote in the midst of violence. In September 2008, Israel's defense minister warned of an impending attack on Gaza.[35] The three-week Israeli assault on Gaza in late 2008 and early 2009 was a reminder that peace is not at hand. The domination of Gaza by Hamas and its continued rejection of the two-state solution make the dream of peace seem more remote. The peace process, after all, is predicated on the two-state solution.

HAMAS

In December, 1987, a leaflet was distributed after Friday prayers at mosques throughout the West Bank and the Gaza Strip. The leaflet, entitled "The Blessed Uprising," appeared less than a month after the start of the December 1987 intifada, or uprising. Signed the Islamic Resistance Movement, Palestine, or "Harakat Al-Muqawamah Al-Islamiyyah, Falasteen," Hamas was announced to the world. The leaflet concluded with the statement, "Let the Intifada continue with strength for the sake of justice, freedom, pride and honor."[36] It was amazing to see one of my shy, reserved, and very religious students distributing the leaflets with energy and enthusiasm. He suddenly became a political activist. His new group, Hamas, did not start the intifida but it was born out of it. Its roots, however, go much farther back in Palestinian history.

Hamas takes root in the Palestinian branch of the Muslim Brotherhood. Originally, the Brotherhood was founded in Egypt. A high school teacher named Hassan al-Banna founded the Egyptian revivalist movement. Al-Banna attempted to create a pure religious party that advocated the application of Islamic teachings in commerce, social welfare, education, and even physical fitness. In early 1928, al-Banna founded the Muslim Brotherhood to carry out such programs. The Brotherhood started many such programs including cooperatives, schools, sports clubs, and even military education programs. The Brotherhood emphasized that ignorance is unIslamic and a good Muslim must receive education.[37] In 1936, the Brotherhood gained attention when it sent volunteers to Palestine to help Palestinians fend off the threat against them from British colonialism and Zionist plans. That move contributed to the rise of the Palestinian branch of the Muslim Brotherhood. It was that branch of the Brotherhood that declared the creation of Hamas in late 1987.

The Palestinian branch of the Brotherhood began with a number of small groups in many communities. By 1943, a national branch was formed under the name of the Makarem Society of Jerusalem. The participation of Palestinian delegates at the Fifth Convention of the Muslim Brotherhood in Aleppo, Syria, in 1944 is a clear indication of the existence of a Palestinian branch.[38] A central office of the Muslim Brotherhood of Palestine was officially inaugurated on May 6, 1946, in the presence of many Palestinian notables and official leaders. By early 1948, the Brotherhood grew in membership and visibility. Its public mobilization campaigns were clearly anti-Zionist and called for jihad against the ruling British authorities and the Zionists. The Brotherhood remained active among the Palestinians after the birth of Israel. Suppressed by Egyptian authorities in Gaza and Jordanian ones in the West Bank, the Brotherhood limited its activities to religious education and the application of Islamic law in personal and civil matters. By the late 1980s, the Brotherhood decided to add its strength to resisting the occupation.

Hamas began with the short-term goal of resisting Israel's occupation. Its long-term objective, however, is to establish an Islamic state in all of historic Palestine. Its operations are divided into two major programs. The social program works to build infrastructures like schools, hospitals, orphanages, and mosques. The other, a militant program, carries out acts of violent resistance and is called the Izz al-Din al-Qassam Brigades. It is this militant arm of Hamas that carried out several suicide bombings in Israel and spearheaded the rocket firing from Gaza into southern Israel.

Palestinian leaders engaged in the peace process view such acts with disdain, for they bring about harsh response from Israel's mighty military machine and derail negotiations. When Hamas decided to run for the Palestinian Legislative Council in 2006, it ushered in a power struggle that remains with us to this day. Hamas defeated Fateh in that election. Ismael Haniyyah, a prominent Hamas leader, became the Prime Minister only to face tough sanctions by Israel and its allies. Now, the power struggle between Fateh and Hamas was in full swing. By May 2007, Hamas fighters were able to overcome the security forces in Gaza and take over. Palestinian authority President Abbas promptly ousted the Hamas cabinet and the Palestinians under occupation fell to two authorities. The West Bank became Fateh run and Gaza fell to Hamas's rule.

Under Hamas, life in Gaza became more orderly, but Israel's tight blockade made it more difficult. Palestinian rocket fire into Israel and Israeli raids into Gaza continued to provide fuel for an eventual explosion. That came about in late December 2008 and lasted for three weeks into 2009. By the time Israel halted its operations, more than 1,400 Palestinians were killed, most of them civilians. The Gaza Strip was devastated and now will require years to rebuild.

In the meantime, Israel had an election in February 2009. The result was a victory for the right-wing parties committed to continue building settlements on the West Bank. With Fateh and Hamas refusing to engage each other, and Israel preferring land over peace, a two-state solution seems farther away than ever.

CHAPTER 4

NORTHERN IRELAND, IRAQ, AFGHANISTAN, AND OTHER CONFLICTS

Terrorism is not limited to one region in the world. It is truly global, but its root causes are often similar. In this chapter, we will take a look at the use of terrorism in a variety of areas around the world. The Northern Irish conflict generated terrorism for generations. Terror in Colombia has ravaged that country as it did in Chechnya and Congo. The American occupation of Iraq and Afghanistan gave birth to atrocities there as well.

Northern Ireland presents a nationalist conflict where violence and terrorism were employed as tools in the struggle between the parties involved. Similar to the Palestinian struggle, the Irish resistance had limited resources to face the overwhelming power of its opponent. Consequently, it used violence and terrorism to resist the greater violence and terrorism heaped on it by the occupying power. Globalization also played a role in the Irish struggle. Similar to the Palestinian struggle, the violence was often aimed at a global audience. Support from others abroad strengthened the resistance movement. Just like the struggle of the Palestinians, the struggle of the Irish is misperceived as another conflict between religious antagonists rather than national ones. Consequently, the global community tends to explain the violence in Northern Ireland as irrational behavior of religious extremists. This chapter discusses the conflict in Northern Ireland and other cases and shows how they are conflicts over national rather than religious rights. While the Northern Irish conflict has a religious aspect because the two protagonist groups identify themselves by religious labels, it is essentially a conflict between the British and the Irish and is based on a belief that Northern Ireland was illegally occupied by Britain. This chapter also describes the migration of dreams and nightmares between the British and Irish in regard to both sides' hopes and terrorist acts.

HISTORICAL BACKGROUND

Irish history dates back to about 6000 B.C.E., when the first European settlers came to the island's northeastern coast and moved inland along riverbanks. Around 4000 B.C.E., Celtic tribes from Britain invaded Ireland and gained control of the island. The Celts divided the island into kingdoms called *tuatha*, which in time fought each other over boundaries.[1]

During the latter part of the eighth century, Vikings in search of riches and slaves began committing terrorist raids, creating settlements on the southern and eastern coasts of Ireland. Viking sieges were extremely vicious, as towns were systematically attacked nearly every year through the eighth and early ninth centuries. Towns such as Clonmacnoise, Clonfert, Seir, and Birr of central Ireland were burned to the ground, while prominent monasteries such as Holmpatrick, Inishmurray, Inishbofin, and Sceilg Mhicil were also destroyed. Many settlements were harbors and became Ireland's major towns, including Cork, Dublin, Limerick, and Waterford. A united group of princes of several kingdoms under the leadership of the Irish king Brian Boru defeated the Vikings at Clontarf in 1014. But the problems of outside invaders were not over for the Irish people.

In the 1160s, the Norman king of England, Henry II, sent volunteers to help the king of Leinster, Dermot MacMurrough, regain his throne.

Richard FitzGilbert de Clare, in league with MacMurrough, sacked Wexford in 1169 and attacked and seized Waterford. By the time King Dermont died in 1171, the Norman volunteers had taken over the kingdom and named a Norman baron as the new king. In that same year, the barons recognized the king of England, Henry II, as lord of Ireland. By the fourteenth century, the Normans had control over all of Ireland. Their loyalty to the British Crown, however, began to fade as time went on. The British monarchy wanted none of that. In 1534, King Henry VIII decreed direct rule over Ireland. In 1541, he forced the Irish Parliament to declare him king of Ireland. English settlers were given confiscated Irish lands to create what was called the "plantation of Ireland." Soon after, Henry's daughter Elizabeth outlawed Roman Catholic services and attempted to impose Protestantism in Ireland. The Irish rebelled. Their revolts in the late 1500s under the leadership of Shane O'Neil and later Hugh O'Neil are major landmarks in Irish history. The British Crown, nonetheless, was too strong and was able to put down the revolt by 1603.

By 1641, the Irish rebelled again. Their rebellion lasted eight years but was brutally crushed by Oliver Cromwell, who eventually brought in more Protestant Englishmen to settle on confiscated Irish lands. Tens of thousands were killed as a result of Cromwell's terrorist attacks— many died during massacres or through mass starvation. Thousands were forced into slavery and sent to the American colonies and the West Indies. Irish Catholics were also stripped of their civil rights, as the practice of Catholicism was outlawed. By 1704, the Catholic Irish held only a seventh of the land in their own country. They were also subject to a severe system of apartheid where they were excluded from the Irish Parliament and military service.

In time, it was the Protestants of Ireland who began to demand change. Unhappy about tight British control over the island and the limited powers of the Irish Parliament, many Irish Protestants began to demand a greater role in their own governance. The British consequently gave the Parliament more powers, which, in turn, gave Catholics some more rights. Catholics were permitted to hold property, and their religious rights were granted. The all-Protestant Parliament did not grant Catholics political rights. But some Protestant Irish began to demand equal rights for all the people of Ireland. They formed a group called the United Irishmen, which demanded independence from

Britain. In 1798, they rebelled. The rebellion, best known for the Catholic uprising in Wexford, was crushed.[2] Many of the rebels were peasants—poorly armed, they had no chance of defeating the British Empire. In total, it is estimated that as many as 30,000 Irish died during the rebellion.[3] Shortly thereafter, the British Parliament passed the Act of Union. Under this act, Ireland became a part of the United Kingdom. As a part of the United Kingdom, the Irish Parliament was dissolved in 1801, and Ireland fell again to direct British rule. But Irish representatives now served in the British Parliament.

Under British rule, Ireland's economy experienced a decline while the population grew. In time, poverty became commonplace. A potato plant disease between 1845 and 1847 contributed to what became known as the Potato Famine, killing as many as one million as a result of starvation and illness.[4] The famine had much more severe economic consequences in the southern part of Ireland than it did in the north. This was a result of the fact that the southern part was kept predominantly agrarian, while the north was encouraged to industrialize. Some have questioned whether the British colonization and subjugation of the Irish exacerbated the effects of the famine.[5] British landowners controlled a majority of agricultural land in Ireland, relegating Irish peasants to lives as indentured servants. In their pursuit of profits, the British aristocracy actually exported food from Ireland during the famine—food that Irish peasants were too poor to afford. In the midst of the famine, British Prime Minister John Russell also cut off all aid to Ireland, reflecting the belief that it was not a British responsibility to provide for the oppressed. Millions of Irish migrated to the United States as a result of the famine.

The difficult times, coupled with the disparities between the south and the north, gave rise to calls for home rule. Many Protestants feared the idea of home rule, as it might mean a Catholic Parliament. Failure to achieve home rule contributed to the rise of new organizations. In 1905, Sinn Fein was founded and dedicated itself to the idea of home rule. Meaning "We Ourselves," Sinn Fein did not advocate complete independence from Britain. The Irish Republican Brotherhood, however, founded around the same time, did insist on total independence from Britain. With the rise of an organized independence movement, events eventually began to unravel.

In 1914, the British Parliament, fearing the power of independent forces, passed a home rule law. Home rule, though, was slowed down with the outbreak of World War I. The Irish Republican Brotherhood saw the war as an opportunity to achieve independence from a Britain that was too busy with its European engagement. Under the leadership of Patrick Pearse, the Republicans began a rebellion on Easter Monday 1916, also known as the Easter Rising. For weeks, Republicans, determined to achieve independence, fought British troops who were equally determined to prevent it. Eventually, the British defeated the rebels, although at great cost. The terror committed that day resulted in the destruction of a large part of Dublin as well as the deaths of over 250 civilians.[6]

As punishment for the Easter Rising, the British government executed fifteen of the leaders of the rebellion. The executions enraged many Catholics and strengthened the Republican cause. With their enhanced image, the Republicans were now able to take control over Sinn Fein. Consequently, in the 1918 election, Sinn Fein won 73 of Ireland's 105 seats in Britain's Parliament. The newly elected parliamentarians refused to go to London to take their seats in the Parliament. Instead, they met in Dublin, calling themselves the Irish House of Deputies. Fighting immediately broke out and continued for many years.

With fighting raging in Ireland, the British Parliament passed the Government of Ireland Act in 1920, which went into effect in 1921. The new law divided Ireland into two separate states that were to remain a part of the United Kingdom with some form of self-government. The northern state consisted of six counties with a Protestant majority. The second state consisted of twenty-six other counties, mostly in the south, with a Catholic majority. The northern six counties accepted the act and declared Northern Ireland as part of the United Kingdom. The leaders of the southern parts wanted nothing less than independence. Fighting for independence was carried out by the Irish Republican Army (IRA), which attacked British installations in their areas. Negotiations between the IRA and the British in 1921 led to an agreement that gave southern Ireland the status of a British dominion under the name of the Irish Free State. On April 18, 1949, the Irish prime minister, John A. Costello, cut all Irish ties with Britain and declared the country independent.

THE CONFLICT OVER NORTHERN IRELAND

The partition of Ireland created a Northern Ireland that incorporated six counties with a Protestant majority. Northern Ireland continued to send representatives to the British Parliament, where ultimate authority was held. The local government in Northern Ireland had authority over education, policing, social services, and municipal affairs.

The IRA saw the partition as an illegal act that took away part of their Ireland. They continued their struggle for a united and independent Ireland. Their struggle often took the shape of terrorist attacks on British and Northern Irish institutions. To fight terror, the Northern Irish and British created an almost exclusive Protestant police force. The Catholics of Northern Ireland, numbering about a third of the population, were caught in a vicious cycle of violence and discrimination, suffering an assault on their civil liberties under draconian emergency legislation issued by the British and Northern Irish.[7] A system of economic sanctions was also introduced that purposely discriminated against the Catholics.[8]

In sum, the first phase of the Northern Irish struggle aimed at unity and independence. Led by the IRA, this phase lasted for more than three decades and included violence and terrorism as well as passive resistance. The years of this phase of the Irish struggle contributed to a greater polarization between the Protestant majority and the Catholic minority in the north.

The second phase of the struggle centered on civil rights rather than unity with the south. This did not mean that unity with the south was no longer an aspiration; rather, the discrimination against Catholics became so severe and entrenched that it took priority over the long-term objective. By the 1950s, many Catholics in Northern Ireland were ready to replace their goal of unity with the south with a new goal of equality in Northern Ireland. By January 1964, Patricia and Don McLusky created a new organization and pushed for fairness in "housing, public appointments, electoral practices, boundaries, and employment."[9] This group eventually gave rise to the Northern Ireland Civil Rights Association (NICRA) in 1967. NICRA aimed at immediate social reforms rather than long-term issues of unity with the rest of Ireland. It demanded reforms that would end job discrimination and housing inequities, promote electoral honesty, and end emergency legislation.

NICRA was modeled after the London-based National Council for Civil Liberties and imitated the activities of the civil rights movement in the United States. Its campaign involved protest marches, sit-ins, and a heavy use of the media to educate the public of its position and about the grave inequities in Northern Ireland.

Clearly, the rise of a Catholic middle class in Northern Ireland contributed to a shift in tactics. Civil disobedience replaced armed struggle to achieve desired ends. Equal rights also took precedence over nationalism. NICRA and its supporters played a part in the migration of dreams, joining the American and Native American civil rights movements in spreading the message that extremism and terrorism are not viable responses to repression.

The civil rights movement achieved some successes. Several of its objectives were met. Unfortunately, they were short lived. The fact that the movement was overwhelmingly Catholic scared the Protestant population. Many Protestant loyalists saw the movement as an attack on their own privileges. Consequently, they treated it as a threat to their supremacy and attempted to destroy it. This led to growing disorder as the civil rights activists were met with both official and vigilante violence. The repression drove some members of the movement to extremism and to violence. This combination made it difficult for the local administration to keep order. Therefore, in 1969, the British sent in troops to maintain law and order. The Catholic population originally welcomed the troops, but soon they perceived them as a British attempt to preserve an unfair status quo.

The British reoccupation of Northern Ireland ushered in the third phase of the Irish struggle. A newly formed Provisional IRA (PIRA) began a campaign of armed struggle and terrorism to rid the territory of British occupation troops. In 1971, the government of Northern Ireland introduced internment as a tool to stop the violence. The failure of internment led the British to invoke their powers under the Government of Ireland Act and suspended the local government in favor of direct British rule. A secretary of state for Northern Ireland now ruled the territory on behalf of the United Kingdom. A Northern Ireland office ran the government's ministries, and the Protestant unionists lost control for the very first time since 1920.

The year 1972 was the bloodiest in Northern Ireland's violent history. One such incident that must linger in the memories and history books of the Catholic minority is commonly known as "Bloody Sunday." The events of that day caused shock and revulsion around the world and resulted in a dramatic increase in support for the IRA and its struggle to reunite Northern Ireland with the rest of Ireland. On Sunday January 30, 1972, a NICRA march took place in Derry to protest internment and to demand political and social equality for Catholics in Northern Ireland. Tens of thousands of people, including children, took part in that protest. The British Army prevented the marchers from entering the city center, and many marchers moved to another area to hold a rally. Some marchers began throwing stones at the British soldiers. The soldiers responded in a deadly fashion, killing thirteen protestors and injuring thirteen others. The soldiers insisted that they had come under fire from the IRA prior to their firing back. The participants in the march insisted that no shots were fired at the soldiers. Much speculation still surrounds this issue. But one thing is certain: if British soldiers were guilty of committing the massacre on that day with which many charge them, it would undoubtedly constitute an act of state terrorism. Whatever may have caused the violence, the consequences of Bloody Sunday led to a new wave of violence and enhanced support among the Catholic population for the IRA at the expense of the civil rights movement.

The cycle of violence prompted the British government to look for alternatives. A new political accommodation that would control the violence required co-optation of the Catholic minority. In order to do so, the British sought a greater role for that community in the government of the region. Second, they needed to create a vision for the future that maintains Catholic links to Ireland. They did so by creating the Council of Ireland, an intergovernmental and inter-Parliamentary level between Northern Ireland and the Republic of Ireland.

The period between 1972 and 1993 witnessed the emergence of a low-intensity conflict that involved three distinct parties. The army, local recruits, and the police force represented the British. A militarized PIRA and smaller groups, such as the Irish National Liberation Army, espoused the Catholic cause. The Protestants of Northern Ireland had loyalist paramilitaries that included the Ulster Defence Association/Ulster Freedom Fighters (UDA/UFF) and the Ulster Volunteer Force (UVF). Violence and terrorism among the various groups had become commonplace. State responses to the violence by the other groups often led to human and civil rights violations, inflaming the situation even more. Between 1972 and 1995, more than 3,500 people had been killed in the violence.[10] Given the small population of Northern Ireland (1.6 million), this figure is rather significant.

Violence and terrorism proliferated by the loyalist paramilitaries and British government forces[11] and by the PIRA and smaller groups have contributed to the migration of nightmares throughout the United Kingdom. Patrick Finucane is one of the many victims in this conflict. A Belfast lawyer, Finucane was murdered in front of his family by loyalist paramilitaries as punishment for his investigation into the killing of human rights lawyer Rosemary Nelson (also perpetrated by the loyalists). Patrick's wife Geraldine, along with many others, blames the British Royal Ulster Constabulary (RUC) police force for allegedly participating in the loyalists' killings:

> It is clear that the British Government is responsible for the deaths of my husband and Rosemary Nelson. Pat and Rosemary were the victims of British Government policy—that of selective targeting and directed assassination. My journey to this conclusion has taken eleven years, and having arrived at this point I am not only convinced by what I have learned, but I am also horrified by it because the truth as I now know it to be is overwhelming. I have observed first hand the whole period of the conflict in the North of Ireland, from having lived through it and having had its worst horrors visited upon me and my family. Like everyone else, I yearn for a peaceful society in which to live.[12]

The RUC has even been accused of torture. David Adams was awarded £30,000 by a high court in Ireland after it was shown that RUC officers lied in court about their torture of Adams at the Castlereagh Holding Center. All told, British officers broke two of his ribs and a leg and punctured his lung.[13] Sadly, many human rights violations such as those mentioned here go unpunished in Irish and British courts.

The IRA has also been implicated in terrorist acts such as car and building bombings as well as torture. The stories of Sean Dunlop and James McCommack reveal much about the practices of the IRA. Dunlop, originally expelled from Northern Ireland by the IRA, was beaten by some of its members on his return to his home in Belfast. Photos of his injuries revealed that his elbows, wrists, legs, ankles, feet, and many toes were broken.[14] Another victim of IRA attacks, McCommack describes the suffering he has endured throughout the years:

> I, and so many like me are the innocent victims of IRA activity. What we have suffered as a result of IRA terrorism is unforgivable. . . . As a part-time member of the Ulster Defence Regiment, I was on patrol in the Whitecross area [Northern Ireland] when our Land Rover came under attack by gunfire. I was thrown around and received an injury to my left foot. In recent times I had to attend the doctor with terrible pain in my foot, which has over the years got worse and worse. My foot is now riddled with arthritis. . . . My cousin Joyce Bryans died leaving a husband and two small children. Not for long the IRA murdered him at Kingsmills and left his children orphans. On the same night I was on duty and was called to the scene. Bodies lay piled on the road where they had been shot. I will never forget it. . . . I could go on and on, I have lost so many good friends and relatives to the IRA.[15]

SOLUTIONS TO VIOLENCE IN NORTHERN IRELAND

Persistent violence has further polarized the two main communities of Northern Ireland. It has wreaked havoc into the economy and created a human tragedy. The British government made many attempts to find a solution to the violence, but it became entangled in the violence as well, and its attempts to find a solution ended up in vain. In the two decades between 1974 and 1994, there were seven British attempts at a solution. All failed in the face of Irish opposition. Consequently, the British role became limited to the containment of violence.

In frustration, the British attempted another route to ending the violence in Northern Ireland. In 1985, the British government reached an agreement with the Republic of Ireland giving it a consultative role in Northern Ireland's affairs. The agreement reintroduced Ireland as a permanent partner in the Northern Irish conflict. This Anglo-Irish Agreement paved the way for increased security cooperation between the two countries. Symbolically and legally, the agreement recognized a legitimate role for Ireland in Northern Irish affairs. It also indicated Irish acceptance of the existence of a state of Northern Ireland and of its right to remain part of the United Kingdom if the majority so wished.

The Anglo-Irish Agreement ushered in a new era in the Irish struggle, which slowly entered into its fourth phase. While many Protestant Northern Irish were outraged that the agreement was negotiated in their absence, the Catholics in Northern Ireland generally welcomed it and saw in it a British willingness to recognize their aspirations for ending the conflict in a manner that recognizes their Irish heritage. In fact, the agreement showed a British recognition of the validity of both Protestant unionist and Catholic Republican aspirations. The agreement, as well as the subsequent legislation aiming at dealing with the inequality in education and employment, paved the way for further changes of attitudes toward a peaceful resolution to the long conflict. At long last, the era of armed struggle was being replaced with an era of diplomatic and political struggle.

THE PEACE PROCESS

Historically, the Irish conflict has been a dispute concerning sovereignty and identity. The Protestant unionist majority wanted to remain in union with Britain, and the growing Catholic Republican minority wanted to maintain their Irish identity and connection. Each side believed that their cause was just. In the process, both sides committed atrocities that make it hard for the other to forgive or forget. The British therefore managed to create a historic tragedy next door as they did throughout their colonial empire in centuries past. Now, they are trying to pick up the pieces and find a meaningful solution that will settle the issues and relieve them of further responsibility.

By the late 1980s, a number of developments took place to help make a peace process possible. First, the Anglo-Irish Agreement was signed, recognizing the aspirations of both parties to the conflict. Second, the debate within the Catholic IRA's ranks was settled in favor of those who questioned the utility of an attrition strategy. The new leaders favored a peacemaking model. Third, a similar movement in favor of a political solution took place within the Protestant paramilitary organizations. Finally, the rise of the Irish Americans to key government and business positions in the United States helped moderate their positions toward more pragmatism and political compromise.

Secret contacts between the British government and the IRA in 1990 paved the way for the peace process. In 1992, the Northern Irish government also started secret discussions with Sinn Fein. In late 1994, the British and Irish governments issued the Downing Street Declaration stressing the right of the Northern Irish to self-determination, including their right to join a united Ireland on the basis of consent.[16] The declaration aimed at an IRA cease-fire declaration. It also required an Irish constitutional change recognizing the acceptance of consent as the legal basis for Irish unity.

The IRA did issue a declaration of "complete cessation of military operations" in 1994. Protestant paramilitary groups followed suit a few months later. At the same time, the British and Irish governments agreed on a framework for future negotiations. The stage was now set for a comprehensive settlement of the conflict. But the British government's slim majority in Parliament slowed down the progress. By 1996, the peace process seemed doomed to failure over issues of disarmament. Violence soon replaced negotiations as the IRA called off its cease-fire and Protestant groups insisted on holding inflammatory parades in Catholic areas. The 1997 election of Prime Minister Tony Blair with a large majority gave the peace process new life. Sinn Fein was brought back into the negotiations. An American, George Mitchell, was reengaged as the chairman of the negotiations. The negotiations bore fruit in April 1998. The Good Friday Agreement was reached, and all the parties signed on to five major provisions. First, the citizens of Northern Ireland will hold the future constitutional status of their territory. Second, unity could occur if the people of Ireland, north and south, vote for it. Third, Northern Ireland's current position will remain as part of the United Kingdom. Fourth, the people of Northern Ireland could identify themselves as Irish, British, or both. Fifth, Ireland would drop its territorial claim to Northern Ireland and redefine the Irish nation in terms of people rather than territory.[17]

The Good Friday Agreement was ratified by referendums in both Ireland and Northern Ireland. The process for a peaceful resolution in Northern Ireland did face some setbacks, however. Most of those revolved around the issue of decommissioning or disarmament. Fear and suspicion continue to hamper progress. But on July 28, 2005, the IRA announced that it was relinquishing violence and giving up its arms. Consequently, a power-sharing government was put in place in May of 2007. The road map to peace, therefore, has been set as a point of no return. Just as the Palestinian armed groups ended up negotiating, Northern Irish armed groups saw a similar result. In neither place has peace been finalized, but in both the process of reconciliation has started—with varying results still to be seen. In other cases, such as Congo, Chechnya, and Colombia, that process is some distance away.

THE CASE OF AMERICAN-COLOMBIAN TERROR

Colombia has been plagued by terrorism for many years, although some aspects of the conflict remain hidden from foreigners. While the kidnappings, murders, and bombings of the Colombian guerillas (FARC and ELN) are widely focused on by the American media, the atrocities of the government and its affiliates remain generally hidden. Colombian paramilitaries, which work hand in hand with the Colombian military, are responsible for some of the most atrocious human rights violations in recent times. Simultaneously, the U.S. government is supporting the paramilitaries through Plan Colombia, which allocates billions of dollars supposedly to fight the Colombian drug trade.[18] While Plan Colombia is justified under the rhetoric of fighting the Colombian cocaine trade, the reality is that the spraying of defoliants, as done to eliminate coca crops, is one of the least effective means of fighting drug abuse.[19] This, coupled with the admission in the U.S. media that Plan Colombia has failed to limit the Colombian drug trade, indicates that there is an ulterior motive explaining American intentions. A more likely reason for Plan Colombia is the use of the Colombian military and paramilitary groups to destroy the guerilla movements in order to end the threat posed by the guerillas to the Colombian government and U.S. hegemony in Latin America. By 2008, the U.S. government had invested $4 billion into Plan Colombia. On March 1, 2008, the Colombian troops entered neighboring Ecuador and killed FARC leader Raul Reyes.

Such an assault on the guerillas has cost the Colombians much, as the migration of nightmares has taken hold of the masses of the Colombian people. Paramilitary groups target more than the guerillas in their assault. Suspected guerilla supporters and sympathizers have been the victims of paramilitary massacres.[20] Human Rights attorney Josué Giraldo is one example. While playing in front of his home with his two daughters, he was gunned down by paramilitaries. Human rights monitor Blanca Cecilia Valero was also murdered by paramilitaries in retaliation for her network's printing of an editorial that criticized the U.S. shipment of weapons to the Colombian government.[21] Sadly, these two examples are not isolated incidents. Colombian paramilitaries and guerillas have been responsible for the deaths of thousands of individuals in their war for control of the nation.[22]

TERRORISM IN THE RUSSIAN-CHECHEN CONFLICT

The Russian government has come under serious criticism for its human rights violations in its war to eliminate the Chechen separatist movement. Brutal Russian repression has been employed in order to crush the separatist rebellion directed from Chechnya. Chechen rebels have also drawn criticism because of their reckless suicide bombings on Russian targets, much like the Palestinian suicide bombings in Israel and the occupied territories. Russian troops have been condemned for acts including torture, summary executions, bombings in civilian areas, multiple massacres, disappearances, and various other human rights violations.[23]

Islam Dombaev, Murat Lyanov, and Timur Tabzhanov all have one thing in common: they are all listed as "disappeared" after they were detained by the Russian government. On June 28, 2000, Islam left his house to meet up with his friend Murat as they both traveled to Timur's home to play the guitar. Sometime during the night, all three boys were stopped and detained by Russian troops under the control of the Ministry of Internal Affairs. The boys were taken to a local military camp and then sent to an unknown location where their parents were unable to find them. When the boys' parents asked for information about their sons' detainment, law enforcement officers answered with lies, giving them the runaround; some demanded money for the return of the children, but none ever followed through. The reactions of the boys' parents are crucial in that they show the desperate position in which they found themselves, victimized by a corrupt police force and unable to find any relevant information on the status of their children.[24]

Residents of Chechen towns have also been terrorized in the Russian government's bombing campaigns. Civilians in the town of Grozny, for example, have been subject to deplorable human rights violations.[25] Magomet Usamov, a resident of one Grozny suburb and eyewitness to the bombings, explains that they were so severe that he and his friends and family were not even able to get water from the local community water tank, as it had been destroyed by Russian bombing. Traveling to a dam near his home, a bomb fell near Usamov's path. "Two women died right before my eyes," he explains the terror of that day: "Their bodies flew up into the air, then fell back onto the pavement. I was about 200 meters away from the explosion, and it left a crater about six meters deep. People are too terrified to even poke their noses outside."[26]

Chechen rebels have also terrorized the Russian people, taking hostages and carrying out suicide bombings against trains, theaters, government buildings, and other public areas. In one such instance, Chechen forces took eight hundred hostages at the Moscow theater, ending in the deaths of over one hundred people.[27] Grandmother to one of the hostages, Yekaterina Ostankhova describes her experiences during the conflict: "It's a nightmare. . . . What's next? This is the capital of all places. I've come here and I've heard nothing. I'm just standing here. I'd be willing to go inside, even if they kill me."[28]

Chechen separatists have been quick to define the conflict as a struggle for independence, while Russian authorities have classified it as a campaign to stop Chechen terror. Both sides have committed terrorist attacks, and both sides view their use of force as legitimate and necessary. The Russian government has used the War on Terror to step up its repression of the Chechen people. Chechen rebels have used increased international interest in the conflict to call attention to the Russian government's atrocities. Stronger criticism, in the end, will be necessary to pressure the Russian government into curtailing its human rights abuses. Conversely, secession may be the only concession that will please many of the critics of Russian violence.

Highlighting the violence in the Russian-Chechen conflict, human rights organizations such as Human Rights Watch and Amnesty International have made strong efforts to stimulate condemnation of the human rights violations on both sides. Both organizations have played an important role in portraying the severity of the Russian-Chechen conflict on a global scale, and in this respect both contribute to the migration of nightmares by relaying victims' stories and Russian-Chechen human rights violations throughout the world. This, nonetheless, may have positive implications for the promotion and protection of universal human rights. It is possible that, in the future, these organizations will become even more important in promoting the migration of dreams across state borders and in forming nonviolent solutions to terrorist conflicts.

By 2009, Chechnya had become calm and began major reconstruction projects. Chechens, however, continue to pay a terrible human price in torture and targeted killing of suspected insurgence activists. Many Chechens are still living in diaspora and the future of the region continues to hang in the balance. Calm could turn into violence at any time.

TERRORISM IN AFRICA: THE CASE OF CONGO

Decades of corrupt leadership and civil war have plagued one of the hardest-hit and most violent nation-states today, the Democratic Republic of the Congo. Such conflict, predictably, has been accompanied by an incredible amount of death and suffering by the Congolese people. A brief review of the nation's history is essential in order to understand the persistence of violence and terrorism in Congo today.

HISTORICAL BACKGROUND: 1960–2003

Congo received its independence from Belgium in 1960, only to fall victim to another power struggle between the remaining Belgian forces, the Belgian-populated province of Katanga, and the new government of President Joseph Kasavubu and Prime Minister Patrice Lumumba. The Congolese central leadership also faced threats from the United States. Prime Minister Lumumba was considered an enemy of the United States for what were considered by American leaders to be his "Communist" political leanings.[29] In the end, Lumumba was assassinated during the coup of Mobutu Sese Seko, who had served as a lieutenant under Lumumba's administration. It was eventually shown that the United States, more specifically the Central Intelligence Agency, had been one of the main supporters of the military overthrow.[30]

Mobutu went on to rule Congo for over thirty years, renaming the country Zaire. The majority of the people of Zaire lived in extreme poverty during this period, while the Mobutu regime went on to plunder the nation's abundance of natural resources, violently subjugating any resistance that emerged through his own "reign of terror."[31] Mobutu's thirty-year rule was accompanied by significant weakening of the Zairian state as well as massive economic decline.

By the early 1990s, Mobutu's power had severely weakened—his regime held power only through massive repression and foreign aid. Mobutu eventually stepped down in 1997 after popular rebellion against his dictatorial rule. Such a significant step toward democracy, unfortunately, has not been accompanied by national peace and prosperity. In the following years, Congo (renamed in 1997 after Mobutu's fall) fell victim to a conflict between regional powers, such as Angola, Rwanda, Uganda, and Zimbabwe, all of which desired to justify their presence in Congo by supposedly "promoting African mediation of the Zairian internal conflict."[32] In reality, it is more likely that they have used Congo's misfortune in order to exploit the nation's natural resources.

Mobutu's rule was followed by that of Laurent-Desire Kabila, a Congolese warlord who, on assuming power, proceeded to abolish the nation's constitution and establish his own dictatorship. Kabila's rule remained similar to that of Mobutu, as he ignored the plight of the nation's poor and attempted to enrich his own financial standing. Conflict during this period was also expedited by the massive influx of foreign refugees from the conflicts in Rwanda and Burundi. Perhaps one of the most important events, though, was the 1998 rebellion against Kabila, supported by Rwanda and Uganda, which touched off a renewed civil war in Congo. Kabila's attack on the rebels provided the necessary pretext for Zimbabwe, Burundi, Angola, Uganda, and Rwanda to intervene in the conflict. Kabila was eventually assassinated in 2001, leading to the takeover of the presidency by his son, Joseph Kabila, who was equally unsuccessful in ending the now international conflict in Congo.

TERROR IN CONGO

The human casualties as a result of Congo's continued civil war are striking. Some estimates predict that the conflict has resulted in the deaths of over 3.3 million people and the displacement of tens of thousands of others and led to widespread malnutrition.[33] Rape is widespread and continues with impunity, further expanding the presence of sexually transmitted disease throughout the nation. Children soldiers have been recruited on all sides as well. In fact, the situation is so desperate that over 12 percent of Congolese children do not reach the age of one.[34]

Human Rights Watch has done extensive documentation of the victims of the Congolese conflict. Some of the stories they have identified are enlightening for those attempting to understand the severity of this conflict. The account of one woman who was raped by RCD (Rwandan-backed Congolese Rally for Democracy) soldiers explains her experiences after the rape in detail: "Afterwards I went home. I tried to hide it from my husband but he found out. He said that I accepted it voluntarily. He said this although I had bruises and marks where the soldiers had pressed their fingernails into my inner thigh." In another example, another woman raped by a Rwandan soldier attempted to obtain help from her pastor, although to no avail:

> When I got home, I went to the pastor to tell him what happened. His wife heard the conversation and went around and told everyone about it. Now I am an outcast. No one will come to see me or share anything with me. My second husband said he was unlucky with wives because he had already lost two wives before me. We don't get along. Sometimes he says I should go back to [my first] husband . . . or I should go be with another man.[35]

The stories told here reinforce more than just the brutality of various armed forces in Congo; they also reveal the extreme sexism that has prevailed in this conflict, as women who are the victim of sexist violence are further demonized by their husbands and communities, only to suffer indefinitely as if they were guilty of committing some crime against humanity.

The recruitment of child soldiers as young as seven years old by the Kabila government as well as by the RCD forces has constituted another disaster accompanying the Congolese conflict. Kabila had such forces from 1996 through the following years despite promises by his government to end the practice of recruiting children. Living conditions for child soldiers are reported to be atrocious, as many are underfed and underclothed, not to mention suffering the trauma of participation in brutal conflict at such an early age.[36] Three boys, for example, had been enlisted against their will in 1997, 1998, and 1999 at the ages seventeen, thirteen, and sixteen. Although two of the boys were related, they had been recruited at different times, one on his way home from school and the other from church. Both ended up in the same training camp; both were able to escape. According to one of the boys, "They gave us wooden sticks shaped like guns—if you lost it, you'd be killed. We were shown real guns and how to work them but they always took them back later. Only when you got to the front were you given a gun." The first time the two boys attempted to escape, they had been severely beaten. Such a punishment was not the worst, though, as the boys remembered one boy who had been killed for trying to escape the camp.[37] Another thirteen-year-old boy who was picked up described his experiences during abduction and training:

> "I was coming from school at about 5 P.M. I went to school in the afternoon. I was heading home when soldiers in a vehicle stopped me and made me get in. They were Rwandans. There were lots of other young boys in the vehicle. . . . We were all ten, twelve, thirteen years old and older. Then we were sent to Camp . . . and trained there. Lots were killed in the training. Lots died of sickness. The food was poorly prepared and many got dysentery.[38]

Far from the standards and expectations in First World countries such as the United States and the United Kingdom, Congolese children and adolescents are often forced into dreadful conditions in which no youth should have to suffer. They are subject to appalling psychological attacks, subjected to the brutality of warfare at tremendously early ages.

Without the existence of any meaningful rehabilitation programs and with the continuation of this conflict, it is unlikely that the people of Congo, especially its women and children, will ever see the light at the end of the tunnel. Some have argued that an international peace-keeping force is needed in order to help quell the conflict. Others have argued that international intervention may serve as a catalyst to provoke more conflict. Either way, Congo stands at the forefront of the African nations that have been plagued by violence, initiated during colonial domination and persisting through the period of independence. The conflict represents the brutality of the globalization of civil conflicts as the nation-states of Africa, motivated like other nations subscribing to power politics, have undertaken one of the most deadly terrorist wars in human history.

THE IRAQ WAR AND THE "WAR ON TERROR"

Hardly a year after the attacks of September 11, 2001, former president George W. Bush announced that Iraq possessed and produced weapons of mass destruction and must be disarmed.[39] His vice president had claimed there was an Iraqi threat even earlier when he stated "there is no doubt that Saddam Hussein now has weapons of mass destruction."[40] Soon after, U.S. troops along with their British allies invaded Iraq in a wave of "shock and awe" that took the nightmares of September 11, 2001, to a country that had no ties with that event. By the start of 2009, more than one hundred thousand Iraqi civilians had been killed and about four million had become refugees. The country's infrastructure was so damaged that the average daily electricity supply to an Iraqi home dropped to less than two hours, while 70 percent of Iraqis have no access to adequate water supplies.

While the George W. Bush administration claimed the war on Iraq was part of its "War on Terror," the fact remains that the Iraqi regime at the time was secular and anti-Islamist. Iraq was then more open than most Islamic countries. Its laws were based on Western and Arab nationalist tenets. Its people enjoyed more rights than most in the region. Religious minorities were protected and citizens had an array of civil liberties so long as they did not oppose the Ba'ath regime under the leadership of Saddam Hussein. Those who dared oppose the regime were dealt with severely through an array of secret services and tough measures. But the United States did not wage war on that regime because its people lacked political rights; it did so under the faulty pretext of fighting terrorism.

There are many theories as to why the Bush administration turned its powerful military machine toward Iraq. Many people in Arab and Islamic countries believe that the Bush administration was motivated by its determination to control oil sources in the Middle East. Iraq, being a leading exporter of oil with plenty of reserves, would come under U.S. control. Another belief in Arab and Islamic countries has to do with the protection of Israel. After Iraq invaded Kuwait on August 2, 1990, the United States led an international war to liberate that tiny neighbor of Iraq. During the war, Iraq launched missile attacks against Israel. Fearing that the missiles were equipped with chemical weapons, Israel distributed gas masks to its citizens. When Iraqi Scud missiles hit, the Israeli population was terrified. While Iraq's missiles did not directly kill any Israelis, the trauma of an Arab regime attacking the heart of Israel left its mark on the psyche of the country as a whole. Many in Islamic and Arab circles believe that the United States acted against the regime to eliminate such a threat to Israel's security. After all, many Arabs and Muslims are convinced that Israel dominates U.S. policy in the Middle East.

Many U.S. and European analysts argued that the Bush administration was misguided in its claim that Iraq's Saddam Hussein had weapons of mass destruction. Time has proven them right, as no such weapons were found in Iraq by the teams of inspectors sent to the country. Iraq may have had the intention and the capability to develop nuclear weapons but did not. In the 1980s, Iraq had chemical weapons and used them against its Kurdish rebels. It also used them against Iran in the eight-year war between the countries in the same decade. Few Western commentators argued that George W. Bush wanted to finish the war his father had started. Back in 1991, George H. W. Bush had waged a war against Iraq to liberate Kuwait. Once Kuwait was liberated, the United States was satisfied with sanctions against the Iraqi regime. But a number of politicians and commentators felt that the United States should have gone all the way to Baghdad. Once the younger Bush became president, he wanted to complete the task of overthrowing the Ba'ath regime, especially after the discovery of a failed Iraqi attempt to assassinate his father on one of his visits to Kuwait.

The Bush administration, of course, made a number of arguments in support of a war against Iraq. The "weapons of mass destruction" excuse was the official one. But the president and his cohorts also argued that Iraq supported al Qaeda and terrorism. That argument is both incorrect and accurate. Iraq did not support al Qaeda but it was a strong supporter of Palestinian suicide bombers against Israel's occupation of Palestinian lands. In fact, Iraq paid the families of Palestinian suicide bombers the sum of U.S.$25,000 to rebuild their homes after Israel retaliated against them by destroying the homes of their families. Saddam Hussein himself often praised those Palestinians as heroes.

The Bush team more convincingly promoted the tactic of taking the war on terrorism to the terrorists. Here, the Bush administration calculated that by occupying Iraq, al Qaeda and its supporters would come to Iraq rather than the United States to fight the Americans. As we know, that they did. In the process, terrorism was fueled and tens of thousands of Iraqis and thousands of Americans were killed. An entire country with no culpability for the September 11 attacks was destroyed for generations to come. Al Qaeda itself became a major beneficiary of that war as people the world over saw the United States as a hegemonic occupier.

Another less convincing argument put forth by the Bush administration to justify its war on Iraq used the rhetoric of democratization. Early in his presidency, George W. Bush referred to Iraq, Iran, and North Korea as the "Axis of Evil." He attacked Saddam Hussein's regime as dictatorial, one that threatened its own population. By invading the country in 2003, the Bush administration was liberating the Iraqis from their dictator. While Saddam Hussein was an authoritarian leader, he was not the only one in the region. If the United States is to take upon itself the task of ridding the region of all such regimes, it would have to fight some of its close friends there.

American troops are not the first to enter Iraq after victory. In 1917, the British did so as well. General Stanley Maude made a speech to the Iraqi public as he entered Baghdad. In that speech he told the people of Iraq, "We come to you not as conquerors or enemies, but as libera-tors."[41] When the British finally withdrew from Iraq in 1932, they left behind a cemetery with the remains of 33,000 British soldiers. Most of the Iraqis who were killed during the vicious insurgency had been de-termined to rid the homeland of foreign troops. History is there for us to learn from, rather than repeat.

Regardless of the reasons U.S. troops were in Iraq or our leaders' in-tentions for the future of the country, many in Iraq and the Middle East region harbor vivid memories of foreign occupiers. Many also believe that the United States invaded the country for its oil resources rather than its oppressive regime. In a recent visit to the region, I was told over and over that the United States will never leave Iraq and will surely cre-ate permanent military bases there. I hope and pray that they are wrong. The fact remains that such perceptions fuel an indigenous insurgency and play into the hands of extremists flocking into Iraq to fight the Americans. In sum, U.S. military presence in Iraq is counterproductive to the country's political objectives. It simply leads to more terrorism and does not defeat it. Though U.S. soldiers have done a superb job in ending a repressive regime, military leaders tell us there is no military solution for Iraq, only a political one. A fundamental change of course is needed in order for the U.S. and the Iraqis to win the peace.

The war in Afghanistan is definitely tied to terrorism, for it is there that al Qaeda planned and launched the September 11 attacks. That war, which started on October 7, 2001, aimed at routing al Qaeda out of the country and replacing its benefactor regime led by the Taliban. That war still rages and al Qaeda has gone global by decentralizing its operations. Neither the Taliban nor al Qaeda has been totally suppressed.

THE WAR IN AFGHANISTAN

The war in Afghanistan was a response to the September 11, 2001, attacks on the United States. The attacks were planned and carried out by al Qaeda (meaning The Base). Al Qaeda is made up of a group of volunteer fighters who left their home countries in the late 1970s and 1980s and headed to Afghanistan to help in the fight against the Soviet-backed regime there. Known then as the mujahideen, they helped the Afghani rebels wage a valiant struggle against the Soviet soldiers, who had been sent in to rescue the local Communist regime. Ironically, the mujahideen were helped by the American Central Intelligence Agency (CIA). The CIA trained and armed the very same people who later waged the September 11 attacks. Soon after the defeat of the Soviet Union and the fall of the Communist regime, a large number of Arab and other foreign fighters discovered they were not welcome in their own home countries. The governments of those countries feared that the mujahideen would wage domestic regime-change campaigns. After all, the Islamist rhetoric the mujahideen came to use was opposed to such regimes and advocated the creation of a unified Islamic caliphate. Having no country to go back to, many of the foreign fighters in Afghanistan had no option but to remain there.

In Afghanistan, they set up their bases as their new permanent residency. Now equipped with dedication to an Islamist ideology and experience in weaponry, they set out to "liberate" all Islamic societies from injustice and corrupt governments. Injustices against Muslims in Palestine enraged them as did the authoritarian rulers of many Islamic states. U.S. support for Israel and most of the authoritarian regimes in the Arab and Islamic worlds put the Islamists of Afghanistan on a collision course with their former benefactor, the United States. It was in this context that the September 11 attacks were carried out.

The deadly attacks on September 11 shocked the United States as they did the world. The American government responded with an all-out war on al Qaeda and the regime that shielded it, the Afghani government under the Taliban. It did not take long for the Americans and their allies to expel that regime from power and to drive its leaders and the leaders of al Qaeda into hiding. Though the Taliban and al Qaeda were defeated, they were not eliminated. In time, they were able to regroup and carry out attacks against the newly installed pro-American regime as well as against U.S. troops and their allied forces. By 2009, the Taliban and al Qaeda had become a major irritant to stability in the country. More U.S. and allied troops were sent to fight them. Eight years after the September 11 attacks, the top Taliban and al Qaeda leaders remained at large. Many analysts believe that they succeeded in eluding the Americans because the U.S. was bogged down by the war in Iraq.

In both cases, the migration of nightmares created new victims and contributed to a cycle of violence whose end is still unforeseen. The so-called War on Terror has not ended terror. Instead, it has created more terrorism. The financial crisis of 2008 and beyond may very well have been related to the "War on Terror," bringing hardships to people all over the world.

CONCLUSION

This chapter has examined various cases of violence, specifically the British-Irish, American-Colombian, Russian-Chechen, Congolese, and the "War on Terror" conflicts. This examination is necessary to show that terrorism is not a development exclusively in Muslim countries but throughout all nations. The popular conception in many Western countries that the terrorist is a wild-eyed, bloodsucking Arab or Muslim must be buried in order to obtain a more realistic and mature understanding of what fuels terrorism.

Terrorist conflicts most often prevail when one political group, person, or state attempts to assert dominance over other states, areas, and peoples. Terrorism is also a product of desperation in the face of economic inequality and other forms of deprivation. The cases involving Britain, the United States, and Russia are especially important because they reveal how powerful nations rely on terrorist violence to promote specific political goals as well as to establish and maintain regional and worldwide hegemony where possible. The horrors revealed in the stories in this chapter—of the victims of expansionist and imperial terror—serve to remind us of the human consequences that are inseparable from the path of terrorism and violence. In the future, more attention must be focused on the repercussions of terrorism and violence if there is to be any prospect for building more peaceful alternatives to regional and worldwide conflicts.

CHAPTER 5

MIDDLE EASTERN ISLAMIST TERRORISM

The term *Islamist* terrorism is used in this chapter's title, rather than *Islamic* terrorism, for a good reason. Islam is a religion with more than a billion adherents, all of whom can be described as Islamic. But it would be inappropriate to associate an entire religion with the acts of the few. Islamism refers to a political ideology rooted in interpretations of Islam. Just as there are Christian, Jewish, or Hindu fundamentalists who want to determine political action by their religious interpretations, there are Islamists who want to do the same.

In this day and age, it is difficult to talk about the Middle East or Islam in a country such as the United States. Many Americans view both as stereotypes and riddled with ignorance. *Arab* and *Muslim* are often interchanged as if they are one and the same. Images of terrorists, oil sheiks, and camel caravans dominate the popular culture when Arabs or Muslims are discussed. Islam is misunderstood and its teachings often misconstrued. Somehow, Allah is seen as some strange god created by Muslims when *Allah* is simply the Arabic word for God. Even Mohammad, the Messenger of Islam, is attacked and ridiculed. It is natural, then, that this chapter starts with a brief introduction to Islam, the Arabs, and the contemporary Middle East.

ISLAM: ITS TEACHINGS, CONTRIBUTIONS, AND DECLINE

Islam is the by-product of the seventh-century Arabian peninsula. Its story is similar to those of Judaism and Christianity. But unlike Judaism and Christianity, the story of its beginning is a success story. Early Islam succeeded rapidly even during the life of its prophet. Essentially, Muslims believe in the Jewish and Christian legends of creation. The story of Adam and Eve in the Garden of Eden followed by eviction are retold in the Islamic holy book, the Qur'an. They further believe that since their eviction, God has appeared or sent prophets to their descendants in order to bring people back to God's ways. Among those were Abraham, Moses, and Jesus. The stories of all three are highlighted in the Qur'an. But hundreds of years later, God looked around the same region where he sent his beloved prophets to find that most people were still pagan. Therefore, God decided that there was a need for a final message. The angel Gabriel, the same angel who appeared to Mary to inform her of the immaculate conception of Jesus, was sent to earth to relay God's final message. The angel found Mohammad meditating in a cave in the Arabian peninsula and relayed God's message to him. Mohammad spread the message known as the Qur'an to his people despite early persecution.[1] Mohammad succeeded in quickly spreading the message of the Qur'an throughout the Arabian peninsula. Within a hundred years, his followers took the message to distant places, creating in the process a huge empire.

The doctrines and rites of Islam embodied the major features of Judaism and Christianity. They also introduced modifications to them. It is these modifications that gave Islam its Arab character. For example, while Islam retained the idea of looking toward the geographic center in prayer, it changed that center from Jerusalem to Mecca, already an important center of Arab pagan worship. The idea of a holy day was also retained but changed to Friday, the day on which Mohammad achieved his first success. The practice of fasting was also continued but revised and changed to the month of Ramadan. In his way, Mohammad brought monotheism to the Arabs and created a new religion that, despite its spread to distant places and other peoples, has been identified with the national community that first adopted it. Today, the Arabs who are Muslim are a small minority among the Muslims of the world, numbering more than 1.3 billion. The reality of the spread of Islam to Indonesia does much to discredit prevalent stereotypes of this religion. Far from a barbaric country where Islam "prescribes" the subjugation of women, Indonesia has in some ways surpassed the United States in providing important opportunities to women. Indonesians have elected a woman, Megawati Sukarnoputri, to the office of president, something the United States has failed to accomplish in the more than eighty years since women gained the right to vote.

The greatest historical achievement of the Arabs was the globalization of Islam. Islam was carried within a century to distant Indonesia and Spain. As early Muslims conquered the Byzantine Empire, in many cases they absorbed rather than destroyed.[2] In the process, they transformed old knowledge into a distinctive civilization that at its height in the ninth and tenth centuries contributed in many areas to the development of world civilization. In mathematics, Islamic scholars developed the field of algebra and provided the world with the decimal point and its modern numerals. Imagine the budget of the United States using Roman numerals or a computer program without the zero or the decimal point. In medicine, the Islamic Empire had hospitals and was practicing surgery at the time when Europeans were still practicing witchcraft in healing. In the natural sciences, Islamic scientists taught us about physics and the elements. In philosophy, it was Islamic scholars who introduced the works of Aristotle, Socrates, and Plato to a sleeping Europe in its Dark Ages. In sum, the Islamic Empire rivaled the greatest ages of Rome and successfully assimilated and globalized classical literature, Hellenistic philosophy, Byzantine institutions, Roman law, and Syriac and Persian scholarship and art. The result was a creative civilization that contributed immensely to later civilizations. Without the background of the Arab-Islamic contributions, the Renaissance would have been in doubt.

The Arab-Islamic Empire lasted for hundreds of years and spread to distant places, reaching the outskirts of Paris and deep into Central

Asia. By the late thirteenth century, the leadership of the empire went to Ottoman Turks, who led what came to be known as the Ottoman Empire. By the late nineteenth century, the Ottoman Empire had become weak and unable to protect its domain from the advancing western empires.

THE ARABS AND THE CONTEMPORARY MIDDLE EAST

The successes of Islam over the centuries did not prepare the Arabs for their contemporary fate. By the nineteenth century, Islamic societies were clearly far behind those of Europe. The European empires reigned supreme in military power, subordinating the Middle East and the Arab world through the colonial system. Unlike earlier religions, which were forced to cope with defeat and persecution, Islam began with triumphs and victories, a historical experience that seemed to confirm that the Qur'an was indeed God's final revelation. This glorious history has created a dilemma for the modern Arabs who cannot but be aware of their culture's subordination to that of the West.

Some Arab thinkers began to question the relevance of religion to society in the nineteenth century. This process of questioning led to the rise of three distinct schools of thought. All three schools are still with us today. The ramifications of those ideas continue to color events in the region and beyond. The roots of al Qaeda can be traced to the intellectual debate of that era. Essentially, one school of thought argued for adapting Islam to modernity, another advocated a return to what many considered "original Islamic teachings and practices," and a third suggested separating Islam from politics altogether.

The first of these schools of thought, the reform movement, is the brainchild of Jamal al-Din al-Afghani (d. 1897) and Muhammad Abdu (d. 1905). Both were Egyptian intellectuals who taught at al-Azhar University in Cairo. Al-Azhar University is a major center of Islamic study with a long history stretching back to its founding during the golden era of Islam in A.D. 910. Afghani and Abdu believed that the foundations of Islam are still sound and capable of withstanding the stress of modernity. They advocated the exercise of intellect in interpreting Islam. In other words, they suggested more modern interpretations of teachings of Islam. While Afghani and Abdu had some influence in Egypt, their ideas remained confined to an intellectual group that did not come to hold power. However, some of its ideas influenced an Islamist Egyptian party called al-Salafiyya in the early part of the twentieth century. Few of the future members of al Qaeda trace their ideological roots to this early reform movement.

The second wave of ideas came in the form of two distinct movements. The first began in the Arabian peninsula and the other in Egypt. Both movements, while they differ widely, argue for a return to what many considered "proper" Islam and could be called revivalist movements. The Wahhabi school, known as the puritans of Islam, felt that Islam is simple and capable of survival and growth in the modern world if people behave in accordance to its teachings. The school's father, Mohammad Ibn Abdel-Wahhab, advocated a return to Islam as it was practiced at the time of the Prophet Mohammad. Wahhab's teachings found a benefactor in Abdel Aziz Ibn Saud, who attempted to unify the Arabian peninsula under his leadership under the banner of Wahhabism. By the 1920s, Saud created his kingdom over most of the region and enforced the teachings of Wahhab. The Kingdom of Saudi Arabia continues to enforce conservative Wahhabi ideas until this day.[3]

A high school teacher named Hassan al-Banna founded the Egyptian revivalist movement. Al-Banna attempted to create a pure religious party that advocates the application of Islamic teachings in commerce, social welfare, education, and even physical fitness. In early 1928, al-Banna founded the Muslim Brotherhood to carry out such programs. The Brotherhood started many such programs, including cooperatives, schools, sports clubs, and even military education programs. The Brotherhood emphasized that ignorance is un-Islamic and that a good Muslim must receive education. In 1936, the Brotherhood gained attention for its part in the globalization of the British-Palestinian conflict, specifically when it sent volunteers to Palestine to help Palestinians fend off the threat against them from British colonialism and Zionist plans. That move contributed to the rise of the Palestinian branch of the Muslim Brotherhood. It was that branch of the Brotherhood that declared the creation of the Islamic Liberation Movement of Palestine, known as Hamas, in late 1987. Other branches of the Brotherhood also sprung up in many Arab countries. Al-Banna himself did not live long enough to see the fruits of his work. He was assassinated by the Egyptian secret police in 1949. His movement and its many offspring are still a force in

Egypt to this day. It was one of its offshoots that is blamed for the assassination of president Anwar Sadat of Egypt in 1981.[4]

As the reformists and the revivalists were advocating a society based on the teachings of Islam, there were other Arabs who advocated secular nationalism. It was the secular nationalists who came to dominate Arab politics since independence. The secular nationalists are represented by Gamal Abdul Nasser of Egypt, the Ba'athists in Syria and Iraq, and the various Arab kings and presidents who came to power since their countries achieved independence from Western colonial powers.

The nationalists advocated the unity of the Arab homeland. They argued that the creation of the modern Arab states was artificial and reflects Western desires to keep the Arabs divided. Nationalists, such as Michel Aflaq, founder of the Ba'ath Party, explained how the Arabs could not achieve freedom from colonialism and its effects until they are united into their wholesome state. With Israel separating the Arabs of Asia from the Arabs of Africa, unity is not possible.

Socialism is another component of the nationalist agenda. Often called Nasserism, Ba'athism (Arab socialism, the notion of social justice) is embedded in all nationalist agendas. Arab socialism entails land reform to end feudalism; social programs to provide health care, education, and transportation; and nationalization of all natural resources.[5] While the nationalist agenda achieved some early successes, it met with many challenges, leading to a perception of failure. Attacks on nationalist secular leadership by European and American policymakers were almost constant. Liberalization of the economy contributed to further setbacks, and failure in wars with Israel essentially led to discrediting the nationalist forces.[6]

The perceived failure of the secular and nationalists in power contributed to a return to the revivalist approach among many Arabs. The success of the Iranian Revolution in 1979 in overthrowing the U.S.-imposed shah and the rise of the Islamic Republic on the ashes of the old regime gave the revivalists a new life. But it was the Soviet invasion of Afghanistan that gave them the rallying cause.

ISLAMISTS UNITE

When the Soviet Union intervened in Afghanistan in 1979, the United States saw an opportunity to achieve some significant goals. First, the

United States hoped to create a Vietnam-like situation for the Soviet Union. Second, they hoped to create a united Islamic front against the Communist Soviet Union. To do so, the Central Intelligence Agency (CIA) began to recruit and support volunteers from around the Islamic countries to fight in Afghanistan. Consequently, volunteers from Egypt and other Arab countries with Muslim Brotherhood ties or, at least, inclinations joined in with volunteers of the Wahhabi school. It was in bases in Pakistan and at the front in Afghanistan that the union of the two major Arab Islamist schools merged into a single cause. This is when the notion of jihad (holy war) as an international movement of armed pan-Islamic terrorists was born.

It was during the struggle in Afghanistan that Ayman al-Zawahiri, the leading Egyptian Islamist medical doctor, met with Osama bin Laden, the wealthy Saudi Islamist. What united them was the common objective of the "liberation" of Islamic peoples and lands from foreign occupation. The CIA provided $3 billion, including rifles, rocket launchers, mines, and other weapons[7] to over one hundred thousand mujahideen, or Islamic fighters, from forty different countries.[8] The arms and the training they received from the CIA were significant in allowing them to achieve victories against the superior Soviet troops. In the end, thousands of Afghans and Soviet troops died in the conflict. Aside from the effects of torture committed by the mujahideen, half the Afghan people were left disabled, displaced, or dead.[9]

Guerrilla warfare was the method employed by the mujahideen in Afghanistan. Many of the mujahideen died facing the superior Soviet troops. Thus, guerrilla warfare became suicidal in nature. Guerrilla missions were transformed into suicide missions. But with jihad, dying in the cause of liberating Muslims was justified as a heroic act. Thus, the suicide bombers of the future were born. They were the heroes of Afghanistan and became the dream that migrated to Muslim youths in many parts of the world.

The progressive platform of the People's Democratic Party (PDP; the Afghan government at the time of the Soviet invasion of Afghanistan) represented a fundamental threat to the Islamist ideology that mandates the permanent subjugation of women. Before as well as during the Soviet occupation, Afghan women enjoyed more human rights protections than at any other time in history. Unlike past Taliban rule or the Northern Alliance rule of today, during PDP rule, Afghan women enjoyed rights that many Western women have come to take for granted. Afghan women walked through Kabul and other cities without hiding behind the burka; they drove cars, went on dates, enjoyed widespread literacy, attended universities, and studied in fields such as agriculture, engineering, and business and worked as professionals in businesses and in the government.[10] Such rights would be seriously challenged in the face of severe repression by the Taliban and Northern Alliance warlords.

AL QAEDA

Al Qaeda was born out of the struggle in Afghanistan, but its roots go back many decades earlier. The fusion of old revivalist schools of thought gave birth to a new and more militant form of revivalism. Their success in Afghanistan and their feeling of betrayal at the end of that conflict made the new organization and its activists feel a sense of empowerment and provided them with a new cause for which to struggle.

A Palestinian Muslim Brotherhood activist named Abdalla Azzam recruited Osama bin Laden into the struggle in Afghanistan in 1979. Bin Laden, like other recruits, was enthusiastic about the struggle against Communism in Afghanistan. Unlike others, however, he had personal wealth and connections to the Saudi establishment. Al-Zawahiri came to Afghanistan in 1980 from Egypt. He met bin Laden soon after and befriended him. Bin Laden called him "the Doctor" because of his medical degree. During the conflict in Afghanistan, al-Zawahiri worked to save the lives of those mujahideen who were injured. In time, bin Laden drifted away from his old recruiter, Azzam, and closer to his new Egyptian friends, including al-Zawahiri. Those were Islamic Jihad activists and leaders. Their group is the one that carried out the assassination of Egypt's President Anwar Sadat in 1981. The Egyptian Islamic Jihad came out of the Muslim Brotherhood ranks and advocated a militant response to secular leadership in the country.[11]

Al Qaeda was formally founded in 1988, a year prior to the Soviet withdrawal from Afghanistan. Its plans included the overthrow of secular governments and the creation of Islamic ones in Pakistan, Afghanistan, Egypt, and other countries inhabited by Muslim majorities. But their immediate struggle had to do more with protecting Muslims from foreign domination in places such as Afghanistan, Kashmir, and Palestine. In time, that struggle expanded to other places, including Somalia, Chechnya, and Bosnia. As the United States sent troops to Saudi Arabia to liberate Kuwait, Saudi liberation from U.S. troops became another major objective. When the United States and Britain occupied Iraq, the liberation of Iraq became yet one more cause of liberation for which to work.

Al Qaeda's anti-American ideology is not original in that it seeks to challenge American domination of the Middle East—a view that is shared by many throughout the area. What is striking about the organization is its determination to commit terrorist attacks on U.S. soil, something that the majority of Americans never expected before September 11. That aside, bin Laden's brand of Islam is only one interpretation of Islam and is not widely accepted throughout many countries in the Middle East. Bin Laden and al Qaeda's concern with overthrowing the Saudi, Iraqi, and other governments in the region and installing "proper" Islamist ones reinforces a main organizational goal of obtaining political power. Such aspirations show that, far from having altruistic intentions of fighting an "evil empire" and fulfilling the orders of Allah on Earth, bin Laden and other members of al Qaeda are interested in achieving absolute power in order to implement their reactionary political and social agendas. The organization has resorted to indefensible terrorist attacks against unarmed populations in order to force its values and their conceptions of a "legitimate" world order onto usually unwilling peoples.

While the volunteer mujahideen of Afghanistan were supported and armed by the United States, the American bases in Saudi Arabia after the Gulf War, its support of Israel against the Palestinians, and its silence on Chechnya all upset bin Laden and his Egyptian friends in al Qaeda. Now the struggle had to extend to fighting the United States, something the Egyptian cohorts had urged for a long time. What convinced bin Laden to start the campaign against the United States was his sense of American betrayal after the Gulf War. The United States withdrew its support for the mujahideen and, worse, began to pressure Pakistan, Saudi Arabia, and Egypt to crack down on them and their trade in opium. During the Afghanistan struggle, opium had become the mainstay of the mujahideen. Now, the United States not only withdrew its support but also was trying to turn off their lifeline. Moreover, bin Laden's own government of Saudi Arabia invited the United States to establish military bases on its soil. The land of the Prophet Mohammad is now "occupied" by the military of a superpower that is seen as helping oppress Muslims in many parts of the world.

Al Qaeda's refocus on the United States replaced its struggle with the Soviet Union and involved violence by other means. Guerrilla warfare is now global in its reach, and its targets are not only military but also economic and diplomatic. Such attacks by the group and its affiliates began with an attempt to bring down the World Trade Center in New York in 1993. Six people were killed and more than a thousand injured. The United States responded by launching missiles on al Qaeda bases in Afghanistan and targets thought to be related to bin Laden in Sudan. The war had begun.

The war with the United States took the shape of direct attacks on U.S. troops in Somalia, a truck bomb near Saudi Arabia's Khubar U.S. military compound, attacks on U.S. embassies in Africa, and eventually the fateful events of September 11, 2001, and their aftermath. The U.S. response has been even more violent. The United States declared a war on Afghanistan that replaced its Islamist government, conducted a war against Iraq that toppled its secular regime, and carried out constant attacks on Islamists in many parts of the world. Israel followed suit by abrogating its obligations under the Oslo Accords and reoccupied most of the cities of the West Bank and the Gaza Strip. Russia also saw an opportunity to crush the Chechen rebellion by brute force. India also declared its war on terrorism by attacking Islamic rebels in Kashmir. So did Indonesia, the Philippines, Yemen, and many other countries. "War on Terror" became the slogan of suppression and even more oppression against Muslims in many parts of the world.

OSAMA BIN LADEN: BACKGROUND

Osama bin Laden is one of the most notorious individuals in the world today. Born in Saudi Arabia in 1957 to a Yemeni father and a Syrian mother, he was the seventeenth of over fifty children fathered by billionaire Mohammed Awad bin Laden. Osama's father made his fortune in a construction business based in South Yemen, sponsored by the Saudi royal family (for which he did many construction jobs). It was from this milieu that Osama bin Laden drew much of his financial resources. When his father died, bin Laden inherited millions, much of which he likely used to fund terrorist attacks throughout the world.

Osama bin Laden studied economics and management at the King Abdul Aziz University in Jeddah, eventually receiving a degree in public administration in 1981. Although bin Laden was brought up in an extremely religious family environment, he gained much of his anti-American ideology from his university studies. Much controversy has recently surrounded bin Laden's family connections, as some have criticized George H. W. Bush, James Baker III, and Dick Cheney for their roles in the Carlyle Group, which has done business with the Binladen Group.

Bin Laden has gained much attention through his support for jihad against secular governments. A major justification for this jihad is the belief that secular governments are illegitimate representatives of Allah on Earth. The Saudi government, the former Soviet Union, and the U.S. government have fallen under attack in this jihad. Attacks from bin Laden and other radical Islamists led the Saudi government to expel bin Laden in 1991 and the United States to make various assassination attempts against him as early as 1998.

AYMAN AL-ZAWAHIRI: BACKGROUND

Ayman al-Zawahiri, nicknamed the "lieutenant," is considered to be one of the main leaders of al Qaeda. Al-Zawahiri was born in 1951 to a middle-class family in Cairo, Egypt. At age fourteen, al-Zawahiri joined the Muslim Brotherhood, an organization devoted to the removing of foreign influences from Egypt. By 1979, he had become a recruiter for Egyptian Islamic Jihad, an organization he eventually became the head of and merged with al Qaeda. Al-Zawahiri was arrested in 1981 after he was suspected in the assassination of former Egyptian President Anwar Sadat, although he was later released because of a lack of evidence concerning his role in the incident. After graduating from medical school, al-Zawahiri traveled to Saudi Arabia, Pakistan, and later to Afghanistan. Al-Zawahiri is wanted in relation to many terrorist attacks, including numerous bombings throughout Egypt; the massacre at Luxor, Egypt, in 1997; and the bombings of U.S. embassies in Kenya and Tanzania. Al-Zawahiri is also suspected to have been involved in the September 11 attacks on the United States, as he is widely believed by many to be in charge of much of al Qaeda's finances.

AL QAEDA AND GLOBAL TERRORISM

One of al Qaeda's main goals is the expulsion of the United States (and any U.S. allies) from Muslim countries and the recreation of an Islamic caliphate encompassing all Islamic societies. Other goals include the end of the state of Israel and the destruction of American-related targets throughout the world (including the United States, as September 11 showed). Al Qaeda has been implicated in many suicide bombings and other attacks, including the 1994 assassination attempt on Egyptian President Hosni Mubarak, the bombing of the World Trade Center in 1993, the 2001 attack on it and the Pentagon, the 2000 bombing of the U.S.S. *Cole*, and other bombings in Saudi Arabia, Turkey, Britain, and Morocco. One of the main reasons al Qaeda poses such a threat is the organization's structure, which is decentralized; many of its "terrorist cells" exist independently from each other and from the organization's leaders. These cells have operated throughout a large number of countries, ranging from the United States and Germany to Kenya, Egypt, Saudi Arabia, and many of the former Soviet republics.

THE UNITED STATES AND AL QAEDA

The relationship between the United States and al Qaeda has been repeatedly marked by violence and inconsistency. The American attacks on Afghanistan and Iraq were justified under the rationale of apprehending Osama bin Laden, head Taliban authorities, and any other al Qaeda members considered to be directly involved with the September 11 attacks. Such attacks against Afghanistan, while succeeding in destroying Afghan towns "too small to be marked on any map," originally[12] have been only marginally effective at apprehending al Qaeda leaders. Osama bin Laden was not captured in Afghanistan, nor was Taliban leader Mullah Mohammad Omar or many top-level al Qaeda members. The connections between Iraq and al Qaeda were unsubstantiated as well. The United States presented no persuasive or conclusive evidence outside of mere speculation that Saddam Hussein had worked with al Qaeda agents.[13] Such attacks on Iraq, then, could only fail in the fight against bin Laden and his terrorist network. An attack on Saudi Arabia, where fifteen of the nineteen September 11 hijackers originated and drew financial aid, may have been a more convincing target than Afghanistan. Ties to the Saudi royal family, however, forced U.S. leaders to consider American oil interests before assaulting this source of al Qaeda's funding and support.

Later attacks on Morocco, Spain, London, Yemen, and Saudi Arabia suggest that the al Qaeda network is still strong. While former President Bush claimed that 65 percent of al Qaeda's leaders have been captured or eliminated so far,[14] he has yet to back his statement up with empirical evidence. Much of the information available suggests that the organization is rapidly growing.[15] One available estimate indicates that, for every one al Qaeda member captured or killed, the organization has been able to recruit two. Every time a terrorist cell is disrupted, another has sprung up in a different location.[16] According to a UN report, al Qaeda may soon obtain biological and chemical weapons of mass destruction.[17] The growth of the organization, along with its possible acquisition of weapons of mass destruction, suggests that more innovative techniques are needed in order to fight al Qaeda and other radical terrorist organizations.

METHODS OLD AND NEW FOR FIGHTING TERRORISM

In order to fight terrorist groups more effectively, it is first necessary for Americans to understand their country's limitations. The notion that American attacks on Middle Eastern nations will eradicate terrorism is, simply put, a myth. In reality, there is no way that the U.S. government can stop many terrorist attacks. For example, there would be little anyone could do if a member of al Qaeda strapped a bomb to himself and detonated it in a public square or on a bus or train. In another instance, should a terrorist group smuggle biological or chemical weapons into the United States, there would be little that any government organization could do to prevent such an attack, for example, on local water facilities. One final example could be an attack on nuclear power plants, many of which have not been properly protected after the September 11 attacks.

A more proactive approach is needed to help prevent future attacks. While the FBI and the Department of Homeland Security should pursue investigations into possible terrorist attacks, these steps constitute more of a short-term solution to fighting terrorism. Long-term solutions are more necessary if the War on Terror is to be truly effective. First and foremost, American leaders and, more important, the American people need to take a look at why so many people in the First and Third World are angry at U.S. foreign policy. American support for repressive governments throughout the world from Saudi Arabia and Kuwait to Israel and Colombia has fueled hostility toward the United States. In turn, many of the world's oppressed view the United States as an accomplice to their governments' gross human rights violations. Americans should also consider the possibility that their government's attacks on civilian populations, as seen in Afghanistan and Iraq, may actually help increase al Qaeda recruiting. Such attacks serve to reinforce the belief in many minds that the United States is one of the primary sponsors and participants in violence and terrorism, that it is one of the largest threats to world peace. Americans should also understand that al Qaeda has likely anticipated a violent American response to September 11 and factored this possibility into its plans to increase its recruitment efforts. This may be an ugly reality, but history suggests that, as in numerous other conflicts, American military responses, rather than weakening the cycle of violence, will actually strengthen it.

Violence should be used only when absolutely necessary to apprehend terror suspects and should be better planned than in past examples, such as Afghanistan, in order to avoid large numbers of civilian casualties. For example, if the United States had evidence proving bin Laden's exact location in a compound or facility, violence could be justified if used in an extremely limited manner to apprehend or perhaps kill him. However, animosity, retaliation, or revenge against the United States could be expected from al Qaeda and other bin Laden supporters. Knowing this, possible retaliation must be a central factor in the decision process, especially if these actions are considered to be just means of capturing or killing bin Laden. Such efforts to apprehend international terrorist suspects, whether they are violent or nonviolent, should be conducted under the jurisdiction of the United Nations. UN control over these operations is essential to minimize the impression that U.S. leaders have no respect for the rules of international law and to demonstrate that the United States is not committed to unilateral aggression (as was shown in the case of Iraq). It must be remembered also that terrorism and religion-based violence is not the monopoly of Islamists. It exists in all faiths.

THE WAR ON TERROR

The U.S. War on Terror took the shape of an invasion of Afghanistan and another of Iraq. It is likely that regime change is an American option in Iran or Syria. All such activities indicate that the United States has linked terrorism almost solely to Islamic countries, the only exception being North Korea. Islamism has produced terror. But religious zealotry has been a major source of terrorism elsewhere. Jewish zealots have been terrorizing a whole people with the support of their government. Hindu terrorists have terrorized Muslims, and Christian terrorists have carried out attacks in many parts of the world, including in the United States. As long as the United States attacks only Islamic zealots and closes its eyes to zealots of other religions, its War on Terror will look like a war on Islam. While the United States can defeat a country or two, it surely cannot defeat a religion. Therefore, it is important to keep the focus on terrorism wherever it occurs and by whoever carries it out.

It is also necessary to reconsider the popular belief, held in nearly all nations, that terrorism is committed exclusively by "other" governments, groups, and peoples. State leaders classify their governments' acts as necessary to protect national security, freedom, and economic prosperity. Such covers, usually taking the form of propaganda, have been overwhelmingly accepted in the United States and other nations. If governments continue to deny responsibility for their violent actions, leaders will continue to pursue terrorist acts with impunity. The dogmatic belief in the sanctity of state intentions and actions must be challenged in order to hold government leaders accountable for illegal and unjust terrorist acts.

Future targets in the War on Terror may not be limited to Islamic countries in the future. Colombian Marxist guerrillas have challenged U.S. corporate dominance in the region as well as U.S. political and strategic interests. Although they challenge U.S. hegemony in Latin America, it is important to distinguish the guerillas from alternate forms of resistance, such as human rights activists, teachers, union workers, and community organizers. These genuine political movements are the main victims of U.S.-sponsored human rights violations in the region and have challenged U.S. political interests at a high enough level to create another major conflict in the eyes of Washington. In this escalating conflict, Colombian guerrillas may be used as the main target in the War on Terror.

CONCLUSION

Islamism has produced terrorism of major magnitude. But Islamism grew out of backwardness and domination. Perhaps the world community would tolerate working with Muslims everywhere to end backwardness and remove sources of oppression. Such an approach to fighting terrorism is more likely to succeed than missiles and violence. Violence of the powerful often sows the seeds of a new form of violence by the oppressed. The dreams of progress and a better life have migrated to Islamic activists, and it is irreversible. The only meaningful response is cooperation for a better world for everyone. Confrontation will lead to more devastation for all. The clash with Islam should be turned into a dialogue with Muslims. After all, al Qaeda does not represent Islamic beliefs as understood by most Muslims around the world. The Obama administration may prove to have the right approach. President Obama's first White House television interview was with al-Arabia, an Arab station. In that interview, he appealed to Arabs and Muslims to start a new chapter based on mutual understanding. Let us hope for success in such endeavors.

CHAPTER 6

CONCLUSION

Both globalization and terrorism have taken center stage in the global struggle for order at the start of the twenty-first century. This book did not intend to present the topics of globalization and terrorism from the perspective only of those who dominate but also the perspective of those who are dominated. In this regard, this is a different kind of book that presents the views of the other. After all, the mainstream scholarship on the subject has often failed us. Why else were we surprised by the events of September 11, 2001? Many scholars assign rights to the powerful while denying the same for those less powerful. The Irish, the Palestinians, and the Islamists all have grievances that are often denied. The violence of the state, whether Nazi Germany, the Soviet Union, or the British Empire, is somehow accepted, while the violence of those dreaming of their own sovereignty is often denied. In this era of globalization, the similarities cannot remain hidden—the double standards have become obvious.

The world has entered the new century through the gates of globalization and found the flames of terrorism flaring inside. Neither globalization nor terrorism is new. Both are as old as society itself. Both processes, though, have radically accelerated over the past hundred years. The process of globalization has grown stronger with the spread of neoliberalism as well as with the globalization of violent and nonviolent government and organizational and individual acts throughout the world. Radical strides in technology, as well as the growth in national leaders' commitment to power politics, have caused terrorism and violence to become more globally destructive than at any other time in history.

A stronger linkage between globalization and terrorism is also a new development. Globalization continues to create new breeding grounds for terrorism by leaving people behind. Because of globalization, a new class of poor and disinherited people is created. But it is because of globalization that this new class knows about its own poverty and dispossession versus the rising wealth and power of the few. The poverty and dispossession, combined with globalization, makes room for the migration of dreams to the minds of the poor. The new dreams often lead to disappointments and frustration. Sometimes the frustration contributes to the violence of the dreaming dispossessed. As the dispossessed carry their violence into the lands of the wealthy, the nightmares of the poor migrate there.

Consequently, dreams and nightmares migrate in both directions. Powerful nations commit terrorist acts against civilians in the name of protecting national security. More often they are aiming at fostering imperial expansion. At the same time, people in the First World are no longer immune to retaliatory as well as aggressive terrorism. This reality is undeniable when considering the terrorist acts of September 11 as well as the large probability that the United States will suffer more terrorism in the future.

Globalization has taken place under the framework of strengthening corporate capitalism throughout all nations of the world. In the emerging global corporate civilization of the twenty-first century, consumers rather than human beings matter. The public good has become subordinate to free trade and corporate drive for profit making. This global setting spawns violence and terrorism, especially when governments become the protectors of corporations rather than the people. The future is likely to bring about more violence and more terror unless modern civilization starts to center on the human being and his or her basic needs. Essentially, that means justice for all those oppressed by foreign or domestic powers. Depending on future events, justice for the oppressed may very well mean a limitation or even an end to short-sighted corporate trade practices, as often seen in the actions of the International Monetary Fund, the World Bank, and the World Trade Organization. It may also mean increased study and awareness on the part of Americans in an effort to better understand the problems plaguing the world's oppressed.

In response to the terror of those terrorized by oppression, governments everywhere are responding violently. Be it wars on terrorism or imprisonment and torture of the terrorists, violence will continue to breed more violence, and the cycle continues. This scenario we are currently living is likely to be viewed by future generations as a sad chapter in the history of humanity. It continues violence without end. Most of its victims are innocent, be they drafted soldiers as happened in Iraq or volunteer soldiers or civilians who happen to be the victims of violence and terrorist aggression. This current situation may not last forever. Other possibilities are there. Let us now take a look at some of them.

WEAPONS OF MASS DESTRUCTION

It is in the realm of the possible, even likely, that the War on Terror, fought against sovereign nations, may very well lead to the proliferation of weapons of mass destruction as well as the increased use of such weapons. After all, biological weapons were used shortly after September 11 in the form of anthrax. We do not yet know who was behind the limited but deadly attacks at that time. Intelligence services in many countries are warning of such a possibility. What they do not warn us about is the possibility of the use of even more destructive weapons of mass destruction by our own government or its allies. Should a more severe terrorist attack take place in a country such as the United States, calls for "let's nuke them" are likely to grow. If in some future war an enemy country uses chemical or biological weapons and kills massive numbers of American or allied troops, it would not be unimaginable if the United States drops a nuclear device on that country. The United States has already done so at the end of World War II and left the door open for such a scenario during its war on Iraq in 2003.

ANTI-AMERICANISM

With or without the use of such destruction at a massive scale, the United States has managed to isolate itself from most people on earth. This growing anti-Americanism is likely to make major leaps with every war the United States engages in. A war on Iran, Syria, or other "rogue" states will further erode the U.S. position in the world. Allied governments will fall under the weight of their own public anti-Americanism. The United States in such a case will feel the global rage because of boycotts of American goods and services. In time, such a scenario, if sustained, will give birth to a new world order.

Corporations in the United States will feel the impact of major global boycotts. Shareholder activism will push corporate America to change course. In its drive for profit, the corporate world may seek to end the cycle of wars and show social, environmental, and human responsibility. If the corporations seize to make profit by exploitation, they will attempt to make profit by any means. Should corporations be pressured enough by the public, they may become more socially responsible.[1]

ATTACKS ON U.S. FORCES ABROAD

A third possible scenario for the future entails continuous attacks on U.S. occupation forces in Iraq, Afghanistan, and possibly Iran. Such a trend has already been witnessed in Iraq, as U.S. troops are subject to guerilla attacks on a regular basis. If such attacks are sustained and if major attacks, such as the one on the Marine compound in Lebanon in the early 1980s, occur, pressure will build up from within the United States to withdraw from the Middle East in general. Such a withdrawal could embolden the anti-American forces and contribute to the fall of pro-American regimes there. Islamist governments are likely to replace many such regimes. This is when Israel is likely to take over the U.S. role, and major regional wars could erupt with some regularity. This scenario is likely to lead to major global economic disruptions.

DEMOCRACY IN IRAQ?

A fourth possible scenario is discussed in Washington, D.C., and elsewhere. This possibility regards chances for a relevant democracy to emerge in postwar Iraq. In some cases, as in Iraq, the Shiite majority is likely to become dominant if majority rule is to be applied. After being suppressed by the Ba'ath regime for so long, the Shiite majority is not likely to accept anything less than majority rule. If they are denied that, they are likely to rebel against any other regime installed into power. Shiite majority rule is likely to be an Islamist one. After all, the religious hierarchy has, in the absence of authority since the fall of the Ba'ath regime, taken the initiative and is reestablishing order in their areas. Many of those are clerics who escaped for protection in the Islamic Republic of Iran during the Saddam Hussein era. They learned the tools that will help them achieve power and maintain order in an Islamist manner. Many argue that the United States will need to remain in Iraq for this democracy to emerge. Many throughout the world, however, see very little chance of the United States supporting a Shiite majority with close relations with Iran, a concern that former Secretary of Defense Donald Rumsfeld has already elaborated on. In addition, a U.S.-imposed privatization of Iraq and its resources will likely make democracy impossible, as anyone familiar with democracy knows that it is the right of the Iraqi people rather than their occupiers to decide what type of government and economic system they will have. Privatization of Iraqi oil will also ensure that the profits from this valuable resource go to corporate stockholders rather than the needy of Iraq. Still, popular pressure placed on American leaders by an educated and active American public, if pursued consistently and vigorously, could provide the necessary impetus for American leaders to concede democratic control to the Iraqi people.

REDISTRIBUTIVE JUSTICE

A fifth scenario has been the dream of activists in the United States for some time. Such a scenario would comprise a more well-informed citizenry that is committed to reinforcing equality, democracy, and the rule of law not only on a national but also on a worldwide level. Such a citizenry could push for a curtailment of the growth of violent American hegemony throughout the world, instead focusing on nonviolent and cooperative solutions to global conflicts. This citizenry could also focus on furthering political and social democracy throughout the United States. Take, for example, the late activist and scholar Eqbal Ahmad. When Dr. Ahmad arrived in the United States, this country was living in an era of racism. Eqbal Ahmad described that era by telling his own story of discrimination and hope in this manner:

> When I went to travel with a Japanese and a Brazilian friend to Memphis, for about four hours, from about 4 P.M. to 8 P.M., we couldn't find a hotel that would admit us because we were colored. One was yellow, one was brown, and one was black. We finally found a place in the ghetto. Exactly two years later, we were integrating the lunch counters and hotels. Just ten years later, I would return to Memphis and stay at the Sheraton Hotel. I want to tell you when I got there, I got out of the taxi, and the bellboy who picked up my luggage was white. I was so happy to see that that I tipped him ten dollars, which I could ill afford, when he brought me to my room. After he left, I sat and cried. The change was marvelous. We still have a long way to go, but change has occurred.[2]

Professor Ahmad, as many activists believe, saw the growing non-white population, coupled with growing pattern of inequality in the United States, as a gleam of hope for radical change in the country. Should such change take place, we are likely to see a modicum of distributive justice in the United States and more emphasis on international law and institutions globally rather than a condemnation of such institutions as seen in the blatantly illegal American war against Iraq. Such grassroots institutions, working under U.S. leadership, would lead efforts to eradicate the desperate conditions that spawn terrorism. These institutions would also focus on cooperation rather than competition and coercion of American allies in fighting the War on Terror. Some argue that the election of President Obama may be a step in that direction. Obama has made it clear that he intends to leave Iraq in a timely fashion and to work collaboratively with Islamic countries to defeat terrorism.

MULTIPOLAR POLITICS, OR, THE END OF THE SINGLE SUPERPOWER

A sixth scenario for the future entails the rise of competitive powers to that of the United States. The European Union could be an alternative.

But the recent enlargement of that union, coupled with the existence of the North Atlantic Treaty Organization (NATO), is likely to prevent such a development. A more likely new alternative to U.S. dominance would be the People's Republic of China. With a fifth of the global population and a continually growing economy, China is destined to achieve superpower status. With the rise of China as a second superpower, the world may witness a refined return to a bipolar system. Poor states would again be able to play one superpower against the other and gain favors for their alignments. The leaders of both superpowers may play off the "threat" of the other in order to justify imperial wars. On the other hand, a bipolar system with increased public awareness and participation in national affairs might curtail the likelihood of indefinite war, as seen in the example of the never-ending War on Terror. A nonaligned movement of the poorer countries would be revived, and some regional conflicts may be intensified, as the competing superpowers would take sides and arm conflicting parties.

Other possible scenarios for the future could be entertained. But the future is not subject to accurate scientific specificity. Change occurs all the time, and when it is revolutionary, it does happen very fast. Past revolutions were not predictable, and future ones are not likely to be either. The world we live in is changing at a dizzying pace. Globalization has become much more rapid than it used to be decades or centuries ago. Terrorism has also become more intense, more deadly, and less selective. Any of us could find ourselves a target of terror, as we all are subject to globalization. Most may not be able to avoid such attacks.

A DREAM FOR THE FUTURE

Before I left my homeland in 1966 to come to study in the United States, I visited my grandparents in their village to say good-bye. I told my grandmother that I was leaving to America to study. Being illiterate, having no television, and having spent all her life in the village, my grandmother seemed to think that I was moving to another city, just like my father had done a few decades earlier. She had no concept of the world, as her village was her own world. Today, the world has come to the village in the form of television, cellular phones, and video and DVD outlets. No more are people living in a village of their own. Now they live in villages and towns of the world.

They have become consumers of corporate productions and products. In the process, old values are crumbling, and global ones are competing to replace them or, at least, refine them.

My grandmother did not know this world. When she passed away, her home was still without running water, and her village was without television. She lived a simple but satisfying life. Now the village has become a part of the city, and the encroachment on simplicity has reached ultimate proportions. The villagers are no longer the same. Their world has been conquered by the globalizing city. Dreams have migrated to the village dwellers who moved to the city to follow their new dreams. The city became so large that it encroached on the village, and the former villager returns as a suburban dweller living on the land of his father. But with him comes even greater dreams of more wealth, more justice, and more consumerism. Also, with him come more violence and less peace and tranquility to the old village.

This book attempted to explain globalization as it relates to terrorism. It argued that globalization has contributed to the migration of dreams. As the gap between expectations and achievement grows, a sense of relative deprivation sets in and contributes to rising violence. As the violence extends beyond the state, it takes with it new nightmares to others living there. Therefore, the migration of dreams from wealthy to poor countries contributes to the migration of nightmares from poor to wealthy ones. Therefore, the nightmares of the Palestinians bring new nightmares to the Israelis, the nightmares of the Northern Irish do the same to the British, and the nightmares of the Islamists carry nightmares to other parts of the world. As long as a sense of deprivation continues to deepen, the curse of nightmares is likely to continue. The nightmare of terrorism is a by-product of the dream of a more equitable world. Should Americans, for example, continue to spend $8 billion a year on cosmetics while the world cannot find the $9 billion it needs to provide people access to clean drinking water and sanitation, the cycle of dreams and nightmares is likely to continue. As the United States spends approximately $500 billion a year on its military, it will likely find itself in a state of endless warfare.

To be heard and empowered, people must have access to the same empowerment tools as everyone else. These include basic needs, such as education, health care, food, and water. People also need to have a sense of being. That sense of being is violated whenever they realize that they are less than equal. When they hear stories about the cloning of a dog or cannot afford a prescription for their dying son or brother who is inflicted with HIV or cholera, they become angry rather than amused. Anger can generate violence.

The world we live in is a web of global interdependence. If the web is too skewed in one direction and uneven, it may be blown away with the wind. A solid web is a well-distributed one. Our world lacks any semblance of distributive justice. The United States stands now as the single power that claims to be global prosecutor, judge, jury, and executioner at the same time. It defines the global economic system, the terrorist, and the ally. It also decides guilt and innocence of all and carries out decisions to punish and reward. As long as the United States continues to defy collaborative efforts and act as the Lone Ranger, there will continue to be growing anti-Americanism and violence against the United States and its interests everywhere. If the new administration in Washington decides to cooperate with others on the basis of international law, the future of all looks better. The dream of a more peaceful world may yet materialize.

Notes

CHAPTER 1   GLOBALIZATION AND TERRORISM

1. Paul Hirst and Grahame Thompson, "Globalization: Ten Frequently Asked Questions," *Soundings* 4 (autumn 1996): 48.

2. Ali A. Mazrui, "Globalization and Cross-Cultural Values: The Politics of Identity and Judgment," *Arab Studies Quarterly* 21, no. 3 (summer 1999): 98.

3. Francis Fukuyama, *The End of History and the Last Man* (New York: Free Press, 1992).

4. Jagdish Bhagwati, "Coping with Antiglobalization: A Trilogy of Discontents," *Foreign Affairs* 81, no. 1 (January/February 2002): 2.

5. Thomas Friedman, *The Lexus and the Olive Tree: Understanding Globalization* (New York: Anchor Press, 2000), 350.

6. Deepak Lal, "The Third World and Globalization," *Critical Review* 14, no. 1 (winter 2000): 45, 36. See also, Martin Wolf, *Why Globalization Works* (New Haven, Conn.: Yale University Press, 2005).

7. Kofi Annan, "Obstacles to Global Progress," *Leaders* 23, no. 2 (April, May, June 2000): 14.

8. Stephen D. Krasner, "Sovereignty," *Foreign Policy*, January/February 2001, 20–30.

9. "Slim in U.S., Big Mac Bulks Up in China," Reuters, September 25, 2002.

10. See, for example, P. J. Taylor, "Izations of the World: Americanization, Modernization and Globalization," in *Demystifying Globalization*, ed. C. Hays and D. Marsh (Basingstoke: Macmillan, 2000), 49–70; Paul Hopper, *Understanding Cultural Globalization* (Polity, 2007); and Lane Crothers, *Globalization and American Popular Culture* (Lanham, Md.: Rowman & Littlefield, 2007).

11. Benjamin Barber, *Jihad vs. McWorld* (New York: Times Books, 1995).

12. Manfred B. Steger, *Globalism: The New Market Ideology* (Lanham, Md.: Rowman & Littlefield, 2002).

13. Quoted in Jan Aart Scholte, *Globalization: A Critical Introduction* (New York: St. Martin's Press, 2000), 16.

14. John Pilger, *The New Rulers of the World* (New York: Verso, 2002), 3.

15. *The Case against "Free Trade": GATT, NAFTA, and the Globalization of Corporate Power* (San Francisco: Earth Island Press and North Atlantic Press, 1993), 195.

16. Michelle Sforza and Lori Wallach, *The WTO: Five Years of Reasons to Resist Corporate Globalization* (New York: Seven Stories Press, 1999), 22.

17. Kevin Danaher, *Ten Reasons to Abolish the IMF and World Bank* (New York: Seven Stories Press, 2001), 32.

18. Danaher, *Ten Reasons to Abolish*, 45, 50.

19. Greg Palast, *The Best Democracy Money Can Buy: The Truth about Corporate Cons, Globalization, and High-Finance Fraudsters* (London: Plume Books, 2003), 153–58. See also Joseph E. Stiglitz, *Making Globalization Work* (New York: W. W. Norton, 2007).

20. Palast, *The Best Democracy Money Can Buy*, 155.

21. Palast, *The Best Democracy Money Can Buy*, 145–46.

22. Working Families in the Global Economy—Who's Losing? http://bernie.house.gov/economy/today.asp#wage. See also Fathali M. Moghaddam, *How Globalization Spurs Terrorism: The Lopsided Benefits of "One World" and Why That Fuels Violence* (Portsmouth, N.H.: Greenwood Press, 2008).

23. "10 Years Later, NAFTA Harvests a Stunted Crop: Rural Mexicans Left Out of Boom," *Chicago Tribune*, December 14, 2003, sec. 1, 1.

24. Noam Chomsky, *Profit over People: Neoliberalism and Global Order* (New York: Seven Stories Press, 1999), 104.

25. Phillips, Peter, and Project Censored, eds., *Censored 2001: 25 Years of Censored News and the Top Censored Stories of the Year* (New York: Seven Stories Press, 2001), 55–59.

26. "Rich-Poor Divide Derails WTO Talks: Potentially Significant Farm Subsidy Not Debated," *CNN.com/World*, September 15, 2003, http://www.cnn.com/2003/WORLD/americas/09/14/wto.talks/.

27. *This Is What Democracy Looks Like* (documentary film), Seattle Independent Media Center and Big Noise Films, 1999.

28. Ted Robert Gurr, *Why Men Rebel* (Princeton, N.J.: Princeton University Press, 1970).

29. Chas W. Freeman, *The Diplomat's Dictionary* (Washington, D.C.: National Defense University Press, 1994), 379.

30. David J. Whittacker, ed., *The Terrorism Reader* (London: Routledge, 2001), 3.

31. Benjamin Netanyahu, *Fighting Terrorism: How Democracies Can Defeat the International Terrorist Network* (New York: Farrar, Straus and Giroux, 2001), 8.

32. Leah Hazard, "Global Recession Reverses 20-Year Trend of Decreasing Poverty," Global Envision, December 24, 2008: http://www.globalvision.org/2008/12/24/global-recession-reverses-20-year-trend-decreasing-poverty.

CHAPTER 2   TERRORISM AND ITS ROOT CAUSES

1. Ali A. Mazrui, "Globalization and Cross-Cultural Values: The Politics of Identity and Judgment," *Arab Studies Quarterly* 21, no. 3 (summer 1999): 98.

2. Jan Aart Scholte, *Globalization: A Critical Introduction* (New York: St. Martin's Press, 2000), 73–74.

3. Immanuel Wallerstein, *The Capitalist World Economy* (Cambridge: Cambridge University Press, 1979).

4. M. Annette Jaimes, ed., *The State of Native America: Genocide, Colonization, and Resistance* (New York: South End Press, 1992), 34.

5. Howard Zinn, *A People's History of the United States: 1492–Present* (New York: HarperPerennial, 1999), 29.

6. Jaimes, *The State of Native America*, 1.

7. Ronald Takaki, *A Different Mirror: A History of Multicultural America* (New York: Back Bay Books, 1993), 228–30.

8. Takaki, *A Different Mirror*, 228–30.

9. Howard Zinn, *Declarations of Independence: Cross-Examining American Ideology* (New York: HarperPerennial, 1991), 96.

10. Adam Hochschild, *King Leopold's Ghost: A Story of Greed, Terror, and Heroism in Colonial Africa* (New York: Houghton Mifflin, 1998), 11, 226, 228.

11. Hochschild, *King Leopold's Ghost*, 225.

12. Zinn, *A People's History of the United States*, 360.

13. "Thousands Pay Respects to Stalin," *BBC.com*, March 6, 2003, http://newsvote.bbc.co.uk/mpapps/pagetools/print/news.bbc.co.uk/1/hi/world/europe/2822029.stm.

14. Zinn, *Declarations of Independence*, 95.

15. John Hersey, *Hiroshima* (New York: Bantam Books, 1986), 46.

16. Hersey, *Hiroshima*, 46, 47.

17. Christopher Hitchens, *The Trial of Henry Kissinger* (New York: Verso, 2001), 35; George C. Herring, *America's Longest War: The United States and Vietnam, 1950–1975* (New York: McGraw-Hill, 2002), 183.

18. Herring, *America's Longest War*, 260.

19. James C. Scott, ed., *Genocide and Democracy in Cambodia: The Khmer Rouge, the United Nations and the International Community* (New Haven, Conn.: Yale University Center for Southeast Studies, 1993), 67.

20. Mark Zepezauer, *The CIA's Greatest Hits* (Chicago: Odonian Press, 1994), 30.

21. Noam Chomsky, *A New Generation Draws the Line: Kosovo, East Timor and the Standards of the West* (New York: Verso, 2000), 20.

22. David Barsamian, *Eqbal Ahmad: Confronting Empire* (Cambridge, Mass.: South End Press, 2000), 96.

23. Marc Herold, "3,500 Civilians Killed in Afghanistan by U.S. Bombs," *Common Dreams Progressive Newswire*, December 10, 2001, http://www.commondreams.org/news2001/1210-01.htm.

24. "Pakistan Readies Forbidding Moonscape of Rock for 10,000 Afghans," *New York Times*, October 5, 2001, B3.

25. "Starving Afghans Set for Biblical Exodus," *Sunday Times* (London), September 30, 2001, 6.

26. Note 37,500 packages for 3.5 million starving Afghans versus 37,500 packages for 7 million starving Afghans.

27. "The Battle for Civilians: Food Packets, Leaflets Carry U.S. Message," *Chicago Sun-Times*, October 9, 2001, 8.

28. "Kay: No Weapons Yet, but Evidence Intent," *CNN.com/Inside Politics*, October 2, 2003, http://www.cnn.com/2003/ALLPOLITICS/10/02/sprj.irq.kay/.

29. "Powell Defends Information He Used to Justify Iraq War," *New York Times*, May 31, 2003, A6.

30. "Rumsfeld Echoes Notion That Iraq Destroyed Arms," *New York Times*, May 28, 2003, A13.

31. Scott Ritter, *Frontier Justice: Weapons of Mass Destruction and the Bushwhacking of America* (New York: Context Books, 2003), 50.

32. Milan Rai, *Regime Unchanged: Why the War on Iraq Changed Nothing* (London: Pluto, 2003), xiv.

33. Howard Zinn, *Terrorism and War* (New York: Seven Stories Press, 2002), 83, 88.

34. Thomas J. Nagy, "The Secret behind the Sanctions: How the U.S. Intentionally Destroyed Iraq's Water Supply," *The Progressive*, September 2001, http://www.progressive.org/0801issue/nagy0901.html; "Brits Fighting Fierce Battles with 1000 Militia Near Basra," Associated Press, March 26, 2003; "Basra Now Military Target, Says UK," *CNN.com/World*, March 25, 2003, http://www.cnn.com/2003/WORLD/europe/03/25/sprj.irq.basra/index.html.

35. Lyford Edwards, *Natural History of Revolution* (New York: Russell & Russell, 1965), 3–4.

36. Brian Crozier, *The Rebel* (Boston: Beacon Press, 1960), 159.

37. *Dawn*, November 10, 2001. Reprinted in Barry Rubin and Judith Colp Rubin, *Anti-American Terrorism and the Middle East: A Documentary Reader* (Oxford: Oxford University Press, 2002), 261.

38. Leila Khaled, "Hakatha Khataft Ta'erat al-Boeing" (This Is How I Hijacked the Boeing), *Shu'un Filastiniyah* 13 (September 1972): 6.

39. Alfred McClung Lee, *Terrorism in Northern Ireland* (Bayside, N.Y.: General Hall, 1983), 162.

40. "Driven by Vengeance and a Desire to Defend the Homeland," *Ha'aretz*, July 16, 2002, 4.

41. Cynthia Brown, ed., *Lost Liberties: Ashcroft and the Assault on Personal Freedom* (New York: New Press, 2003), 33.

42. Nancy Chang, *Silencing Political Dissent: How Post-September 11 Anti-Terrorism Measures Threaten Our Civil Liberties* (New York: Seven Stories Press, 2002), 69.

43. Ephraim Yaar and Tamar Hermann, "Peace Index/Most Israelis Support the Attack on Iraq," *Ha'aretz*, January 16, 2004, http://www.haaretzdaily.com/hasen/pages/ShArt.jhtml?itemNo=269674&sw=public+opinion+polls.

CHAPTER 3   PALESTINE

1. William Quandt, Fuad Jabber, and Ann Mosely Lesch, *The Politics of Palestinian Nationalism* (Berkeley: University of California Press, 1973), 33.

2. Ibrahim Abu-Lughod, "Introduction: On Achieving Independence," in *Intifada: Palestine at the Crossroads*, ed. Jamal R. Nassar and Roger Heacock (New York: Praeger, 1991), 8.

3. Abu-Lughod, "Introduction," 35.

4. For more incidents and details, see Issa Nakhleh, *Encyclopedia of the Palestine Problem* (New York: Intercontinental Books, 1991), 75–85.

5. Great Britain, Foreign Office, *The Political History of Palestine under British Administration: Memorandum to UNSCOP* (Jerusalem: Government Printing Office, 1947), 27.

6. Quoted in John Snetsinger, *Truman, the Jewish Vote and the Creation of Israel* (Stanford, Calif.: Hoover Institution Press, 1974), 75.

7. Harry S. Truman, *Memoirs: Trial and Hope* (Garden City, N.Y.: Doubleday, 1956), 160.

8. Truman, *Memoirs*, 153.

9. Edgar O'Ballance, *The Arab-Israeli War, 1948* (New York: Praeger, 1957), 64.

10. Sir John Baggot Glubb, *A Soldier with the Arabs* (New York: Harper and Row, 1957), 251.

11. Quoted in Fayez A. Sayeh, *A Palestinian View* (Amman: General Union of Palestinian Students, 1970), 4.

12. Qustantin Zuraqa, *The Meaning of Disaster* (Beirut: Khayyat Press, 1956).

13. Odeh P. Odeh, *Masra' Falasteen (The Death of Palestine)* (Jerusalem: Sandukah Brothers, 1950), 30.

14. *Sunday Times* (London), June 15, 1969.

15. For more details on the Israeli invasion, see "Israel in Lebanon: Report of the International Commission," *Journal of Palestine Studies* 12, no. 3 (Spring 1983), 147.

16. Quoted in Arie Bober, ed., *The Other Israel* (New York: Doubleday, 1972), 77.

17. Elfisha Efrat, *Judea and Samaria: Guidelines for Regional and Physical Planning* (Jerusalem: Ministry of Interior, Planning Department, 1970), 1.

18. *L'Express*, May 23–29, 1977, 55. Also quoted in Institute of Palestine Studies, *Who Is Menachem Begin?* (Beirut: Institute of Palestine Studies, 1977), 60.

19. Quoted in Felicia Langer, "Israeli Violations of Human Rights in the Occupied Arab Territories," in *Perspectives on Palestinian Arabs and Israeli Jews*, ed. James J. Zogby (Wilmette, Ill.: Medina Press, 1977), 61.

20. *New York Times*, May 15, 1988, A1.

21. Jim Lederman, "Dateline West Bank: Interpreting the Intifada," *Foreign Policy*, no. 72 (fall 1988): 230.

22. See Zeev Schiff and Ehud Yaari, *The Palestinian Uprising—Israel's Third Front* (New York: Simon and Schuster, 1991), and Don Peretz, *Intifada: The Palestinian Uprising* (Boulder, Colo.: Westview Press, 1990).

23. See Ziad Abu-Amr, *Islamic Fundamentalism in the West Bank and Gaza: Muslim Brotherhood and Islamic Jihad* (Bloomington: Indiana University Press, 1994).

24. For an excellent discussion of the Palestinian position on the conflict over Kuwait, see Ibrahim Abu-Lughod, "Non-Alignment and Commitment in the Gulf Conflicts: Palestine's Policy," *Arab Studies Quarterly* 13, nos. 1–2 (winter/spring 1991): 53–64.

25. Muhammad Hallaj, "U.S. Gulf Policy: Going the Extra Mile for War," *Arab Studies Quarterly* 13, nos. 1–2 (winter/spring 1991): 6.

26. "Main Points of Mideast Peace Plan," *USA Today.com*, http://www.usatoday.com/news/world/2003-05-25-peace-points_x.htm.

27. Benjamin Netanyahu, *A Durable Peace: Israel and Its Place among the Nations* (New York: Warner Books, 1993), 347–48.

28. Roane Carey, ed., *The New Intifada: Resisting Israel's Apartheid* (New York: Verso, 2001), 12.

29. Carey, *The New Intifada*, 13.

30. Both Mizrachi's and Turjeman's stories are from "Erased in a Moment: Suicide Bombing Attacks on Civilians," Human Rights Watch, October 2002, http://www.hrw.org/reports/2002/isrl-pa/ISRAELPA1002-03.htm#P298_35555.

31. Carey, *The New Intifada*, 129.

32. Ramzy Baroud, ed., *Searching Jenin: Eyewitness Accounts of the Israeli Invasion 2002* (Seattle: Cune, 2003), 73–75.

33. Joel Beinin and Zachary Lockman, eds., *Intifada: The Palestinian Uprising against Israeli Occupation* (Cambridge, Mass.: South End Press, 1989), 317, and Jerusalem Media and Communication Centre, "Palestinians Killed during Al-Aqsa Intifada," www.jmcc.org/banner/banner1/listmartyr.htm.

34. Baroud, *Searching Jenin*, 75.

35. *Ha'aretz*, September 19, 2008, 1.

36. From the original document handed to the author at a mosque in Al-Bireh on the West Bank in January 1988.

37. See Richard P. Mitchell, *The Society of the Muslim Brothers*, Oxford: Oxford University Press, 1969.

38. 'Awad Khalil, " Juthoor al-Islam Al-Siyasi fi Falastin" (Roots of Political Islam in Palestine), *Shu'un Filastiniyyah*, no. 227 (February/March, 1992), 19–33.

CHAPTER 4   NORTHERN IRELAND, IRAQ, AFGHANISTAN AND OTHER CONFLICTS

1. For detailed history of Ireland's early years, see S. J. Robert McNally, *Old Ireland* (New York: Fordham University Press, 1965).

2. John Darby, *Conflict in Northern Ireland: The Development of a Polarised Community* (Dublin: Gill and Macmillan, 1976), 5.

3. John Cannon, ed., *The Oxford Companion to British History* (New York: Oxford University Press, 1997), 517–18.

4. Christine Kinealy, ed., *A Death-Dealing Famine: The Great Hunger in Ireland* (Chicago: Pluto, 1997), 148.

5. Kinealy, *A Death-Dealing Famine*, 1–3, and Christine Kinealy, *The Great Irish Famine: Impact, Ideology, and Rebellion* (New York: Palgrave, 2002), 185.

6. "Wars & Conflict: 1916 Easter Rising Insurrection," *BBC News*, http://www.bbc.com.uk/easterrising/insurrection/in03.shtml.

7. "United Kingdom—Human Rights Developments," Human Rights Watch, http://www.hrw.org/reports/1995/WR95/HELSINKI-18.htm.

8. For more details on the numbers of those killed and injured, see Marie-Therese Fay, Mike Morrissey, and Marie Smyth, *Northern Ireland's Troubles: The Human Costs* (London: Pluto, 1999).

9. Alfred McClung Lee, *Terrorism in Northern Ireland* (Bayside, N.Y.: General Hall, 1983), 71.

10. For more details on the numbers of those killed and injured, see Marie-Therese Fay et al., *Northern Ireland's Troubles*.

11. "Northern Ireland—Royal Ulster Constabulary Policing Methods Raise Concern," Human Rights Watch, http://www.hrw.org/press/nire975.htm; "Call for Independent Inquiry into Patrick Finucane's Murder," Human Rights Watch, http://www.hrw.org/campaigns/nireland98/patfin.htm; "Victims of Collusion," Relatives For Justice, http://www.relativesforjustice.com/victims/victims_collusion_a_e.htm.

12. "Hearing: Protection of Human Rights Advocates in Northern Ireland," Testimony of Geraldine Finucane, Commission on Security and Cooperation in Europe, March 14, 2000, http://www.csce.gov/witness.cfm?briefing_id=42&testimony_id=59.

13. "Justice for All? An Analysis of the Human Rights Provisions of the 1998 Northern Ireland Peace Agreement," Human Rights Watch, April 1998, http://www.hrw.org/reports98/nireland/.

14. "Children in Northern Ireland: Abused by Security Forces and Paramilitaries," Human Rights Watch, http://www.hrw.org/reports/pdfs/U/UK/UK927.PDF.

15. "The Story of James McCommack," Families Acting for Innocent Families (FAIR), http://www.victims.org.uk/jimmccommack.html.

16. For more details on the Downing Street Declaration, see Paul Dixon, *Northern Ireland* (New York: Palgrave, 2001), 239–43.

17. See Dixon, *Northern Ireland*, 269–72.

18. "Colombia: Paramilitary Groups Closely Tied to Army, Police: U.S. Funding Military Unit Implicated in Serious Abuses," Human Rights Watch, October 4, 2001, http://www.hrw.org/press/2001/10/sixthdivision.htm.

19. *Z-Magazine Video Series* (documentary film), Plan Colombia, 2003.

20. Robin Kirk, *More Terrible Than Death: Massacres, Drugs, and America's War in Colombia* (New York: Public Affairs, 2003), 182.

21. Editorial, "Killer Networks in Colombia," Human Rights Watch, http://www.hrw.org/campaigns/colomed.html.

22. Matt Kelly, "Colombian General Denies Rights Violation," Human Rights Watch, January 28, 2003, http://colhrnet.igc.org/newitems/jan03/ospina.128.htm.

23. "Chechnya: Human Rights under Attack," Amnesty International, http://www.amnesty.org/russia/chechnya.html.

24. "Human Rights Watch Publications: Detention and Disappearance," Human Rights Watch, http://www.hrw.org/reports/2001/chechnya/Disapfin-02.htm #P354_71196.

25. "Civilians in Grozny Facing Death, Possible Starvation," Human Rights Watch, December 6, 1999, http://www.hrw.org/press/1999/dec/chech1206b.htm.

26. "Civilians in Grozny Facing Death, Possible Starvation."

27. "Russia: Into Harm's Way: Forced Return of Displaced People to Chechnya," Human Rights Watch, January 5, 2003, www.hrw.org/reports/2003/russia 0103/.

28. "Seven Freed from Moscow Theater," *CNN.com/World*, October 25, 2002, http://www.cnn.com/2002/WORLD/europe/10/24/moscow.siege/.

29. Ch. Didier Gondola, *The History of the Congo* (Westport, Conn.: Greenwood Press, 2002), 121.

30. Victor Marchetti and John D. Marks, *The CIA and the Cult of Intelligence* (New York: Dell Books, 1974), 53; William Blum, *Rogue State: A Guide to the World's Only Superpower* (Monroe, Me.: Common Courage Press, 2000), 137–38.

31. Gondola, *The History of the Congo*, 139.

32. Gondola, *The History of the Congo*, 155.

33. "Congo War Zone Awaits French Troops Skeptically," *New York Times*, June 6, 2003, A8.

34. "Innocence of Youth Is Victim of Congo War," *New York Times*, June 23, 2003, A1.

35. "The War within the War: Sexual Violence against Women and Girls in Eastern Congo," Human Rights Watch, June 20, 2002, http://www.hrw.org/reports/2002/drc/.

36. "The Use of Child Soldiers in the Democratic Republic of Congo," Human Rights Watch, http://www.hrw.org/campaigns/crp/congo.htm.

37. "Abduction and Recruitment of Children," Human Rights Watch, http://www.hrw.org/reports/2001/drc3/Goma-05.htm.

38. "Abduction and Recruitment of Children."

39. George W. Bush, "President Bush Outlines Iraqi Threat," White House Website, October 7, 2002, http://www.whitehouse.gov/news/releases/2002/10/2002 10078.html (October 4, 2005).

40. Elisabeth Bumiller and James Dao, "Cheney Says Peril of a Nuclear Iraq Justifies Attack," *New York Times*, August 27, 2002, 1(A).

41. Robert Fisk, "History: For Centuries, We've Been 'Liberating' the Middle East. Why Do We Never Learn?" *The Independent*, March 6, 2003, 4.

CHAPTER 5   MIDDLE EASTERN ISLAMIST TERRORISM

1. For details on Islamic teachings, see John L. Esposito, *Islam: The Straight Path* (Oxford: Oxford University Press, 1991).

2. For a good source on the contributions of the Arab-Islamic Empire, see John S. Badeau et al., *The Genius of Arab Civilization: Source of Renaissance* (Cambridge, Mass.: MIT Press, 1983).

3. See Aziz al-Azmeh, "Wahhabite Polity," in *Arabia and the Gulf: From Traditional Societies to Modern States*, ed. Ian Richard Netton (Totowa, N.J.: Barnes & Noble Books, 1986), 75–90.

4. For more details on the Muslim Brotherhood and its ideology, see Richard Mitchell, *The Society of Muslim Brothers* (New York: Oxford University Press, 1993).

5. For an excellent study on Arab nationalism and its roots, see Rashid Khalidi, *The Origins of Arab Nationalism* (New York: Columbia University Press, 1991).

6. See Michael Hudson, *Middle East Dilemma: The Politics and Economics of Arab Integration* (New York: Columbia University Press, 1999).

7. Mark Perry, *Eclipse: The Last Days of the CIA* (New York: William Morrow and Company, 1992), 325.

8. Michael Parenti, *The Terrorism Trap: 9/11 and Beyond* (San Francisco: City Lights, 2002), 60.

9. William Blum, *Rogue State: A Guide to the World's Only Superpower* (Monroe, Me.: Common Courage Press, 2000), 5.

10. Parenti, *The Terrorism Trap*, 59–60.

11. Paul L. Williams, *Al Qaeda: Brotherhood of Terror* (New York: Alpha, 2002), 76–80.

12. John Pilger, *The New Rulers of the World* (New York: Verso, 2003), 5.

13. "Analysis: Iraq and al-Qaeda," *BBC News World Edition*, October 28, 2002, http://www.news.bbc.co.uk/2/hi-americas/2284123.stm; "Bush Declares 'One Victory

in a War on Terror': He Says Military Phase in Iraq Has Ended," *New York Times*, May 2, 2003, A1; "Report Casts Doubt on Iraq-Al Qaeda Connection," *Washington Post*, June 22, 2003, A1.

14. "Bush Says Attacks on U.S. Forces Won't Deter Him from the Rebuilding of Iraq," *New York Times*, July 2, 2003, A10.

15. "Al Qaeda Links to Saudi Attacks Suggest Network Remains Potent," *Wall Street Journal*, May 14, 2003, A1; "U.S. Suspects al Qaeda in Morocco Bombings: Officials: More Attacks on 'Soft Targets' Likely from Al Qaeda," *CNN.com/World*, May 18, 2003, http://www.cnn.com/2003/WORLD/africa/05/17/al.qaeda.morocco/.

16. "Iraq and Al Qaeda: No Evidence of Alliance," Global Policy, http://www.globalpolicy.org/security/issues/iraq/attack/2003/0219alliance.htm.

17. "U.N. Details al Qaeda Threat," *CNN.com/U.S.*, http://www.cnn.com/2003/US/11/20/un.alqaeda/.

CHAPTER 6   CONCLUSION

1. Noreena Hertz suggests this corporate shift in her book *The Silent Takeover: Global Capitalism and the Death of Democracy* (London: William Heinemann, 2001).

2. Eqbal Ahmad, *Confronting Empire: Interview with David Barsamian* (Cambridge, Mass.: South End Press, 2000), 65–66.

SELECTED

BIBLIOGRAPHY

Albrow, Martin. *The Global Age: State and Society beyond Modernity*. Stanford, Calif.: Stanford University Press, 1997.

Badeau, John S., et al. *The Genius of Arab Civilization*. Cambridge, Mass.: MIT Press, 1983.

Barber, Benjamin R. *Jihad vs. McWorld*. New York: Ballantine Books, 1996.

Baroud, Ramzy, ed. *Searching Jenin: Eyewitness Accounts of the Israeli Invasion 2002*. Seattle: Cune, 2003.

Barsamian, David. *Iqbal Ahmad: Confronting Empire*. Cambridge, Mass.: South End, 2000.

Bauman, Zygmunt. *Globalization: The Human Consequences*. New York: Columbia University Press, 1998.

Beck, Ulrich. *What Is Globalization?* Oxford: Polity Press, 2000.

Beinin, Joel, and Zachary Lockman, eds. *Intifada: The Palestinian Uprising against Israeli Occupation*. Cambridge, Mass.: South End Press, 1989.

Bhagwati, Jagdish. "Coping with Antiglobalization: A Trilogy of Discontents." *Foreign Affairs* 81, no. 1 (2002): 2–7.

Bjorgo, T. *Terror from the Extreme Right*. London: Cassell, 1995.

Black, Jan Knippers. *Inequity in the Global Village: Recycled Rhetoric and Disposable People*. West Hartford, Conn.: Kumarian Press, 1999.

Blum, William. *Rogue State: A Guide to the World's Only Superpower*. Monroe, Maine: Common Courage Press, 2000.

Bourdieu, Pierre. *Acts of Resistance: Against the Tyranny of the Market*. New York: New Press, 1998.

Braman, Sandra, and Annabelle Sreberny-Mohammadi, eds. *Globalization, Communication and Transnational Civil Society*. Cresskill, N.Y.: Hampton Press, 1996.

Brecher, Jeremy, and Tim Costello. *Global Village or Global Pillage? Economic Reconstruction from the Bottom Up*. 2nd ed. Cambridge, Mass.: South End Press, 1998.

Bremer, L. P. *Terrorism: Its Evolving Nature*. Washington, D.C.: Bureau of Public Affairs, 1989.

Brown, Cynthia, ed. *Lost Liberties: Ashcroft and the Assault on Personal Liberty*. New York: New Press, 2003.

Bryan, Lowell, and Diana Farrell. *Market Unbound: Unleashing Global Capitalism*. New York: John Wiley & Sons, 1996.

Buchanan, Patrick J. *The Great Betrayal: How American Sovereignty and Social Justice Are Being Sacrificed to the Gods of the Global Economy*. New York: Little, Brown, 1999.

Burbach, Roger, Orlando Nunez, and Boris Kagarlitsky. *Globalization and Its Discontents: The Rise of Postmodern Socialism*. London: Pluto Press, 1997.

Burns, Timothy, ed. *After History? Francis Fukuyama and His Critics*. Lanham, Md.: Rowman & Littlefield, 1994.

Burtless, Gary, Robert Z. Lawrence, Robert E. Litan, and Robert J. Shapiro. *Globaphobia: Confronting Fears about Open Trade*. Washington, D.C.: Brookings Institution Press, 1998.

Callinicos, Alex. *Social Theory: A Historical Introduction*. New York: New York University Press, 1999.

Cannon, John, ed. *The Oxford Companion to British History*. New York: Oxford University Press, 1997.

Carey, Roane, ed. *The New Intifada: Resisting Israel's Apartheid*. New York: Verso, 2001.

Carnoy, Martin, Manuel Castells, and Stephen S. Cohen, eds. *The Global Economy in the Information Age*. University Park: Pennsylvania State University Press, 1993.

Carroll, William, Radhika Desai, and Warren Magnusson. *Globalization, Social Justice and Social Movements*. Victoria: University of Victoria Press, 1996.

Castells, Manuel. *The Information Age: Economy, Society and Culture*. 3 vols. Oxford: Blackwell, 1996–1998.

Chang, Nancy. *Silencing Political Dissent: How Post-September 11 Anti-Terrorism Measures Threaten Our Civil Liberties*. New York: Seven Stories Press, 2002.

Chase-Dunn, Christopher. *Global Formation: Structures of the World Economy*. Lanham, Md.: Rowman & Littlefield, 1998.

Chomsky, Noam. *A New Generation Draws the Line: Kosovo, East Timor, and the Standards of the West*. New York: Verso, 1999.

———. *9-11*. New York: Seven Stories Press, 2001.

———. *Peace in the Middle East*. New York: Vintage, 1974.

———. *Profit over People: Neoliberalism and Global Order*. New York: Seven Stories Press, 1999.

Clark, Ian. *Globalization and International Relations Theory*. Oxford: Oxford University Press, 1999.

Cohn, Theodore H. *Global Political Economy: Theory and Practice*. New York: Longman, 2000.

Cox, Harvey. "The Market as God." *Atlantic Monthly* 283, no. 3 (1999): 18–23.

Crothers, Lane. *Globalization and American Popular Culture.* Lanham, Md.: Rowman & Littlefield, 2006.

Danaher, Kevin. *Ten Reasons to Abolish the IMF and World Bank.* New York: Seven Stories Press, 2001.

Darby, John. *Conflict in Northern Ireland.* Boulder, Colo.: Westview Press, 1976.

Demers, David. *Global Media: Menace or Messiah?* Cresskill, N.Y.: Hampton Press, 1999.

Derber, Charles. *Corporation Nation.* New York: St. Martin's Press, 1998.

Dixon, Paul. *Northern Ireland: The Politics of War and Peace.* New York: Palgrave, 2001.

Doremus, Paul, William W. Keller, Louis W. Pauly, and Simon Reich. *The Myth of the Global Corporation.* Princeton, N.J.: Princeton University Press, 1998.

Esposito, John L. *Islam: The Straight Path.* Oxford: Oxford University Press, 1991.

Falk, Richard. *Predatory Globalization: A Critique.* Cambridge: Polity Press, 1999.

Featherstone, Mike, ed. *Global Culture.* London: Sage, 1990.

Frank, Andre Gunder. *ReORIENT: Global Economy in the Asian Age.* Berkeley: University of California Press, 1998.

French, Hilary. *Vanishing Borders: Protecting the Planet in the Age of Globalization.* New York: W. W. Norton, 2000.

Friedman, Thomas L. *The Lexus and the Olive Tree: Understanding Globalization.* New York: Anchor Press, 1999.

Fukuyama, Francis. *The End of History and the Last Man.* New York: Free Press, 1992.

———. *The Great Disruption: Human Nature and the Reconstitution of Social Order.* New York: Free Press, 1999.

Gadamer, Hans-Georg. *Truth and Method.* New York: Seabury Press, 1975.

Gardels, Nathan, ed. *The Changing Global Order.* London: Blackwell, 1997.

Gerner, Deborah J. *One Land, Two Peoples.* Boulder, Colo.: Westview Press, 2003.

Giddens, Anthony. *The Third Way.* London: Blackwell, 1998.

Gilpin, Robert. *The Challenge of Global Capitalism: The World Economy in the 21st Century.* Princeton, N.J.: Princeton University Press, 2000.

Gondola, Ch. Didier. *The History of the Congo.* Westport, Conn.: Greenwood Press, 2002.

Gowan, Peter. *The Global Gamble.* London: Verso, 1999.

Gray, John. *False Dawn.* New York: New Press, 1998.

Greider, William. *One World, Ready or Not.* New York: Simon & Schuster, 1997.

Halliday, Fred. "Terrorism in Historical Perspective." *Arab Studies Quarterly* 9, no. 2 (1987): 139–48.

Hannerz, Ulf. *Cultural Complexity.* New York: Columbia University Press, 1992.

Held, David. *Democracy and the Global Order.* Stanford, Calif.: Stanford University Press, 1995.

Held, David, Antony McGrew, David Goldblatt, and Jonathan Perraton. *Global Transformations: Politics, Economics and Culture*. Stanford, Calif.: Stanford University Press, 1999.

Henderson, Hazel. *Beyond Globalization: Shaping a Sustainable Global Economy*. West Hartford, Conn.: Kumarian Press, 1999.

Herman, Edward S., and Robert W. McChesney. *The Global Media: The New Missionaries of Global Capitalism*. London: Cassell, 1997.

Herring, George C. *America's Longest War: The United States and Vietnam, 1950–1975*. New York: McGraw-Hill, 2002.

Hersey, John. *Hiroshima*. New York: Bantam, 1986.

Hertz, Noreena. *The Silent Takeover: Global Capitalism and the Death of Democracy*. London: Random House, 2001.

Hirschman, Albert O. *The Rhetoric of Reaction*. Cambridge, Mass.: Harvard University Press, 1991.

Hirst, Paul, and Grahame Thompson. *Globalization in Question*. 2nd ed. Malden, Mass.: Blackwell Publishers, 1999.

Hitchens, Christopher. *The Trial of Henry Kissinger*. New York: Verso, 2001.

Hochschild, Adam. *King Leopold's Ghost: A Story of Greed, Terror, and Heroism in Colonial Africa*. New York: Houghton Mifflin, 1998.

Hodges, Michael R., John J. Kirton, and Joseph P. Daniels, eds. *The G8's Role in the New Millenium*. Aldershot: Ashgate, 1999.

Holton, Robert J. *Globalization and the Nation-State*. New York: St. Martin's Press, 1998.

Howard, Russell D., and Reid L. Sawyer. *Terrorism and Counterterrorism*. Guilford, Conn: McGraw-Hill/Dushkin, 2003.

Huntington, Samuel P. *The Clash of Civilizations and the Remaking of World Order*. New York: Simon and Schuster, 1996.

Hurrell, Andrew, and Ngaire Woods, eds. *Inequality, Globalization, and World Politics*. Oxford: Oxford University Press, 1999.

Jacoby, Russell. *The End of Utopia*. New York: Westview Press, 1999.

Jaimes, M. Annette, ed. *The State of Native America: Genocide, Colonization, and Resistance*. Boston: South End Press, 1992.

Jameson, Fredric, and Masao Miyoshi, eds. *The Cultures of Globalization*. Durham, N.C.: Duke University Press, 1998.

Kapstein, Ethan B. *Sharing the Wealth: Workers and the World Economy*. New York: W. W. Norton, 1999.

Khalidi, Rashid. *The Origins of Arab Nationalism*. New York: Columbia University Press, 1991.

Kinealy, Christine, ed. *A Death-Dealing Famine: The Great Hunger in Ireland*. Chicago: Pluto Press, 1997.

———. *The Great Irish Famine: Impact, Ideology, and Rebellion*. New York: Palgrave, 2002.

Kirk, Robin. *More Terrible Than Death: Massacres, Drugs, and America's War in Colombia.* New York: Public Affairs, 2003.

Koc, Mustafa. "Globalization as a Discourse." In *From Columbus to ConAgra: The Globalization of Agriculture and Food.* Edited by Alessandro Bonanno et al. Lawrence: University Press of Kansas, 1994.

Korten, David C. *The Post-Corporate World.* West Hartford, Conn.: Kumarian Press, 1999.

———. *When Corporations Rule the World.* West Hartford, Conn.: Kumarian Press, 1996.

Krugman, Paul. *The Accidental Theorist.* New York: W. W. Norton, 1998.

Küng, Hans. *A Global Ethic for Global Politics and Economics.* New York: Oxford University Press, 1998.

Kuttner, Robert. *Everything For Sale.* Chicago: University of Chicago Press, 1997.

Lal, Deepak. "The Third World and Globalization." *Critical Review* 14, no. 1 (winter 2000): 36, 45.

Lechner, Frank J., and John Boli, eds. *The Globalization Reader.* Oxford: Blackwell, 2000.

Lee, Alfred McLung. *Terrorism in Northern Ireland.* New York: General Hall, 1983.

Luttwak, Edward. *Turbo-Capitalism.* New York: HarperCollins, 1999.

Mander, Jerry, and Edward Goldsmith, eds. *The Case against the Global Economy.* New York: Random House (Sierra Club), 1999.

Marchetti, Victor, and John D. Marks. *The CIA and the Cult of Intelligence.* New York: Dell Books, 1974.

Martin, Hans-Peter, and Harald Schumann. *The Global Trap: Globalization and the Assault on Democracy and Prosperity.* New York: Zed Books, 1997.

Mazrui, Ali A. "Globalization and Cross-Cultural Values: The Politics of Identity and Judgment." *Arab Studies Quarterly* 21, no. 3 (1999): 97–110.

McLellan, David. *Ideology.* Minneapolis: University of Minnesota Press, 1986.

McNally, Robert S. J. *Old Ireland.* New York: Fordham University Press, 1965.

Mitchell, Richard. *The Society of Muslim Brothers.* New York: Oxford University Press, 1993.

Mittelman, James H., ed. *Globalization: Critical Reflections.* Boulder, Colo.: Lynne Rienner, 1997.

Moghadam, Valentine M. *Globalization and Social Movements: Islamism, Feminism, and the Global Justice Movement.* Lanham, Md.: Rowman & Littlefield, 2008.

Mokhiber, Russell, and Robert Weissman. *Corporate Predators: The Hunt for Mega-Profits and the Attack on Democracy.* Monroe, Me.: Common Courage Press, 1999.

Munck, Ronnie. *Ireland: Nation, State and Class Struggle.* Boulder, Colo.: Westview Press, 1985.

Nassar, Jamal R., and Roger Heacock. *Intifada: Palestine at the Crossroads.* New York: Praeger, 1990.

————. *The Palestine Liberation Organization: From Armed Struggle to the Declaration of Independence.* New York: Praeger, 1991.

Netanyahu, Benjamin. *A Durable Peace: Israel and Its Place among the Nations.* New York: Warner Books, 1993.

————. *Fighting Terrorism: How Democracies Can Defeat the International Terrorist Network.* New York: Farrar, Straus and Giroux, 2001.

Ohmae, Kenichi. *The Borderless World: Power and Strategy in the Interlinked Economy.* London: HarperCollins, 1990.

————. *The End of the Nation-State.* New York: Free Press, 1995.

Palast, Greg. *The Best Democracy Money Can Buy: The Truth about Corporate Cons, Globalization, and High Finance Fraudsters.* London: Plume, 2003.

Payne, Richard J., and Jamal R. Nassar. *Politics and Culture in the Developing World.* New York: Longman, 2003.

Petras, James. *The Left Strikes Back: Class Conflict in the Age of Neoliberalism.* Boulder, Colo.: Westview Press, 1998.

Phillips, Peter, and Project Censored, eds. *Censored 2001: 25 Years of Censored News and the Top Censored Stories of the Year.* New York: Seven Stories Press, 2001.

Pilger, John. *The New Rulers of the World.* New York: Verso, 2003.

Polanyi, Karl. *The Great Transformation.* 1944. Reprint, Boston: Beacon Press, 1957.

Rai, Milan. *Regime Unchanged: Why the War on Iraq Changed Nothing.* London: Pluto Press, 2003.

Rangan, Subramanian, and Robert Z. Lawrence. *A Prism on Globalization: Corporate Responses to the Dollar.* Washington, D.C.: Brookings Institution Press, 1999.

Rao, C. P., ed. *Globalization, Privatization and Free Market Economy.* Westport, Conn.: Quorum Books, 1998.

Reich, Robert. *The Work of Nations.* New York: Vintage, 1992.

Reinicke, Wolfgang. *Global Public Policy.* Washington, D.C.: Brookings Institution Press, 1998.

Ricoeur, Paul. *Lectures in Ideology and Utopia.* New York: Columbia University Press, 1986.

Ritter, Scott. *Frontier Justice: Weapons of Mass Destruction and the Bushwhacking of America.* New York: Context, 2003.

Ritzer, George. *The McDonaldization of Society.* Thousand Oaks, Calif.: Pine Forge Press, 1993.

Robbins, Bruce. *Feeling Global.* New York: New York University Press, 1999.

Robertson, Roland. *Globalization: Social Theory and Global Culture.* London: Sage, 1992.

Rodrik, Dani. *Has Globalization Gone Too Far?* Washington, D.C.: Institute for International Economics, 1997.

Rorty, Richard. *Achieving Our Century.* Cambridge, Mass.: Harvard University Press, 1998.

Rosenau, James. *Along the Domestic-Foreign Border: Exploring Governance in a Turbulent World*. Cambridge: Cambridge University Press, 1997.

Rubin, Barry, and Judith Colp Rubin. *Anti-American Terrorism in the Middle East*. New York: Oxford University Press, 2002.

Said, Edward W. *The End of the Peace Process*. New York: Pantheon, 2000.

Sassen, Saskia. *The Global City: New York, London, Tokyo*. Princeton, N.J.: Princeton University Press, 1991.

———. *Globalization and Its Discontents*. New York: New Press, 1998.

———. *Losing Control? Sovereignty in the Age of Globalization*. New York: Columbia University Press, 1996.

Schaeffer, Robert K. *Understanding Globalization*. Lanham, Md.: Rowman & Littlefield, 1997.

Scholte, Jan Aart. *Globalization: A Critical Introduction*. New York: St. Martin's Press, 2000.

Scott, Alan, ed. *The Limits of Globalization: Cases and Arguments*. London: Routledge, 1997.

Scott, James C., ed. *Genocide and Democracy in Cambodia: The Khmer Rouge, the United Nations, and the International Community*. New Haven, Conn.: Yale University Southeast Studies, 1993.

Sen, Amartya. *Development as Freedom*. New York: Knopf, 1999.

Singer, Daniel. *Whose Millennium? Theirs or Ours?* New York: Monthly Review Press, 1999.

Smith, David, Dorothy J. Solinger, and Steven C. Topic, eds. *States and Sovereignty in the Global Economy*. London: Routledge, 1999.

Soros, George. *The Crisis of Global Capitalism: Open Society Endangered*. New York: Public Affairs, 1997.

Steger, Manfred B. *Globalism: The New Market Ideology*. Lanham, Md.: Rowman & Littlefield, 2002.

———. *Globalisms: The Great Ideological Struggle of the Twenty-First Century*. Lanham, Md.: Rowman & Littlefield, 2008.

———. *Globalization: A Very Short Introduction*. Oxford: Oxford University Press, 2003.

Takaki, Ronald. *A Different Mirror: A History of Multicultural America*. New York: Back Bay, 1993.

Thomas, Caroline, and Peter Wilkin, eds. *Globalization and the South*. New York: St. Martin's Press, 1997.

Tomlinson, John. *Globalization and Culture*. Chicago: University of Chicago Press, 1999.

Väyrynen, Raimo, ed. *Globalization and Global Governance*. Lanham, Md.: Rowman & Littlefield, 1999.

Wallach, Lori, and Michelle Sforza. *The WTO: Five Years of Reasons to Resist Corporate Globalization*. New York: Seven Stories Press, 1999.

Wallerstein, Immanuel. *The Capitalist World Economy*. Cambridge: Cambridge University Press, 1979.

Waters, Malcolm. *Globalization*. London: Routledge, 1995.

Whittacker, David, ed. *The Terrorism Reader*. London: Routledge, 2001.

Williams, Paul. *Al Qaeda: The Brotherhood of Terror*. New York: Alpha, 2002.

Yergin, Daniel, and Joseph Stanislaw. *The Commanding Heights: The Battle between Government and the Market Place That Is Remaking the Modern World*. New York: Simon and Schuster, 1998.

Zepezauer, Mark. *The CIA's Greatest Hits*. Chicago: Odonian, 1994.

Zinn, Howard. *Declarations of Independence: Cross-examining American Ideology*. New York: HarperPerennial, 1991.

———. *A People's History of the United States: 1492–Present*. New York: HarperPerennial, 1999.

———. *Terrorism and War*. New York: Seven Stories Press, 2002.

Zizek, Slavoj, ed. *Mapping Ideology*. London: Verso, 1994.

Zolo, Danilo. *Democracy and Complexity*. University Park: Pennsylvania State University Press, 1992.

INDEX

About the Author

Jamal R. Nassar is dean of the College of Social and Behavioral Sciences at California State University, San Bernardino. He is the author of *The Palestine Liberation Organization: From Armed Struggle to the Declaration of Independence*, the coauthor of *Politics and Culture in the Developing World: The Impact of Globalization*, and the coeditor of *Change without Borders: The Third World at the End of the Twentieth Century* and *Intifada: Palestine at the Crossroads*.